TIMES *of* REFRESHING

VOLUME 2

TIMES *of*
REFRESHING
VOLUME 2
INSPIRATION, PRAYERS, &
GOD'S WORD FOR EACH DAY

BISHOP JOE IBOJIE &
PASTOR CYNTHIA IBOJIE

CROSS HOUSE BOOKS
Christian Book Publishers
245 Midstocket Road
Aberdeen
AB15 5PH, UK

"The entrance of Your Word brings light."

ISBN: 978-0-9564008-8-8

For Worldwide Distribution, Printed in U.S.A.

1 2 3 4 5 6 7 / 17 16 15 14 13 12

To order products by Dr. Joe Ibojie & other Cross House Books, contact sales@crosshousebooks.co.uk.
Other correspondence: info@crosshousebooks.co.uk.
Visit www.crosshousebooks.co.uk.

Praise Report

B ISHOP Joe and Pastor Cynthia Ibojie have embarked on yet another mammoth task of bringing refreshing times each day from the throne of God through the eternal and living word. Like its earlier volume, this volume of *Times of Refreshing* is divinely inspired and succinctly written. It is packed with spiritual capsules for daily nourishment—wisdom for the moment and encouragement for tough times. This volume of Times of Refreshing marks another significant contribution to victorious Christian living by best-selling author Bishop Joe Ibojie and Pastor Cynthia Ibojie. You will truly be blessed as you daily energize your spirit with *Times of Refreshing Volume 2.*

Dr. Ajee Mamman, President
African and Caribbean Christian Fellowship
Aberdeen, Scotland

Foreword

I am happy to commend this book—*Times of Refreshing Volume 2* to the body of Christ for many reasons. First, I recommend as widely as I can the writings of Joe Ibojie; and second this devotional is unique because it is sharp, brisk, and thoroughly motivational as it is inspirational. Each day's reading leaves you with a lingering memory long after the book is closed.

Start the year with the Spirit-inspired daily nuggets in this book, and as the Bible promises in Psalm 65:11, God will *"crown the year with* [His] *goodness."* This devotional by Joe and Cynthia Ibojie comes out of their life's journey and intimate moments with Jesus. Devotion to Jesus is the goal in any Christian's life. We all know that time is of the essence and we don't always have all the time we need to study in a way we should. The way this devotional is written is to help us whether we have time constraints or not. There are short extracts from the Word of God that leave us with a question at the end that we can continue to meditate on as we go through our day. Meditating on the Points to Ponder will help you to practice the presence of God every moment of each day.

We all know the promise of Jesus, "I will never leave you or forsake you"—journey with the Ibojies during this year and allow yourself to be drawn closer to Jesus in devotion and love. I love what it says about David in 2 Samuel 7:18, it says that David *"went in and sat before the Lord"*; what it means is that he was on his knees sitting back with his face lifted up before the Lord asking Him the question, "Who am I, O Lord God and what is my house?" God had spoken to him about the future of his family and the One who would come, Jesus. David took the time to get before the Lord with what had been said to him.

This devotional will help you in the journey.

I commend this book to you on your life's journey.

Joe Ewen
Founder and Leader, Riverside Church Network
Banff, Scotland, United Kingdom

Introduction

WE are pleased to present this second volume filled with inspiration, love, and hope. As with the first volume, each message was birthed out of our quiet time with the Lord. We allowed each message a time of maturation as it was quintessentially breathed upon and brooded over by the Holy Spirit Himself. This volume like the first volume places high premium on the word of God. God's word has power to deliver from any predicament. A rhema word is the word of God made relevant for your particular situation! It is the word in season for the weary. As you read His word daily, I pray it will lift up from the pages of the book into every fiber of your being, light up your soul, and stir up your spirit. Fill yourself every morning with a word from God before the mundane challenges of life set in. The psalmist says:

> *Direct my steps by Your word, and let no iniquity have dominion over me* (Psalm 119:133 NKJV).

The passage from Second Peter is also succinctly shared in the Message Bible rendition:

> *The main thing to keep in mind here is that no prophecy of Scripture is a matter of private opinion. And why? Because it's not something concocted in the human heart.* **Prophecy resulted when the Holy Spirit prompted men and women to speak God's Word.**

We testify to this truth and confess that perhaps we should claim no ownership of this work but only admit the work of the Holy Spirit who has indeed graciously *"moved and impelled"* us over these several years. Many people have found inspiration and encouragement from these messages, and we pray they will inspire you to greater height in God.

This work is not meant to be a theological treatise nor preaching on doctrinal principles but rather they are messages of inspiration and of hopes for troubled times. As the Bible says, *"I want you to trust Me in your times of troubles, so I can rescue you, and you can give Me glory"* (Ps. 50:14-15 Living Bible). These messages are written to give encouragement and strength to you and so help to build up trust in God in good times and on the day that is evil.

SEEK FIRST THE KINGDOM OF GOD

*But seek first his kingdom and his righteousness, and all
these things will be given to you as well* (Matthew 6:33).

IT is a New Year and a new day! God's infinite grace and mercy abide
to turn things around for a better tomorrow. On our part, one
thing towers above all else—the need to put God first in everything.

As a routine act of life, we should set the things of God as our
highest priority. Priority leads to success and excellence. Good intentions may be wasted if priorities are not set correctly. The key priority
of life must be to seek God because in Him we can find all we need.
What needless burdens we carry all because we don't put God first,
and what needless battles we fight when we don't put Him first!

Points to Ponder

1. Do you routinely place God's will above your own?
2. What does seeking the Kingdom of God really mean?
   What "things" are you hoping God will give to you?

GOD IS THINKING OF YOU!

I'll [God] show up and take care of you as I promised and bring you back home. I know what I'm doing. I have it all planned out—plans to take care of you, not abandon you, plans to give you the future you hope for (Jeremiah 29:11 The Message).

THE above verse is taken from The Message translation of the popular passage in the book of Jeremiah. Key points to note:

- God will definitely show up without fail.
- He is bound by His word to take care of you.
- He will bring you out of any predicament.
- God knows what He is doing.
- God has all things worked out!
- His plan for you is good and gives you a future and hope.

Points to Ponder

1. How sure are you of God's promises to you as stated in Jeremiah 29:11?
2. Do you take comfort in these promises, or do you have doubts in the back of your mind?
3. Can you trust Him fully and have faith in His love for you?

Reading the Bible in a Year: Genesis 3-5 and Matthew 2.

BURNING HEARTS

They asked each other, "Were not our hearts burning within us while he talked with us on the road and opened the Scriptures to us?" (Luke 24:32)

GOD can speak into your spirit, but may withhold your mind from knowing what He said to your spirit. The disciples on the way to Emmaus had this experience. Jesus was in their midst but although they did not recognize Him, they felt a warmth in their spirits—their hearts—as He spoke. Their natural minds failed to comprehend the presence of God in their midst. Is not that true of every one of us? Our spirits may prompt us, yet our minds may fail to recognize the experience. May you never miss the nudging of the Holy Spirit.

Points to Ponder

1. Have you ever felt an inner nudge that your mind tried to ignore?

2. What steps can you take to become more receptive to your spiritual urgings?

BREAKING BREAD WITH FAMILY

So He went home with them. As they sat down to eat, He asked God's blessing on the food and then took a small loaf of bread and broke it and was passing it over to them. When suddenly—it was as though their eyes were opened— they recognized Him! At that moment He disappeared!
(Luke 24:29b-31 Living Bible)

NOTICE this event happened during a family meal that included a seemingly "unknown" guest who was using an ordinary loaf of bread to thank God—then the heavens opened upon them! Things immediately shifted around them! You too can shift things around you for good by obeying the ordinances instituted by Jesus Christ, such as the Holy Communion. Please break bread as often as you can!

Points to Ponder

1. Do you consider Holy Communion a sacred privilege?
2. How many times do you celebrate this breaking of bread at your church?
3. What is your favorite part of the ritual?

GIVE TRUE THANKS TO THE LORD

If I were hungry, I would not mention it to you—for all the world is mine, and everything in it. No, I don't need your sacrifice of flesh and blood. **What I want from you is your true thanks**; *I want your promises fulfilled. I want you to trust me in your times of trouble, so I can rescue you, and you can give me glory* (Psalm 50:12-15 Living Bible).

THESE verses portray the essence of the true worshiper. We were made to worship Him. Thanksgiving is a form worship; the worship of our lips. Give Him thanks today; He inhabits the praises of His people. Hear what the Bible says—the true essence of sacrifice is to test our heart. God lacks nothing and whatever we have comes from Him. But hear a heart cry from the Creator of heaven and earth: *"What I want from you is your true thanks."*

Points to Ponder

1. Have you been routinely thanking your heavenly Father with rote prayers?

2. Do you need to adjust your prayers of thankfulness so they will be "truer"?

_____

_____

_____

GATHERED TOGETHER

O Jerusalem, Jerusalem, the one who kills the prophets and stones those who are sent to her! How often I wanted to gather your children together, as a hen gathers her brood under her wings, but you were not willing! (Luke 13:34 NKJV)

WE are in the end times and these are days that Jesus warned about thousands of years ago. These days are upon us! The key wisdom is to apply the long-revealed truth to our hearts so we will not go astray! Truly, the heart without God is wicked to say the least. The dangerous mindset of perpetuating wickedness, killing people, and man's inhumanity against man and thinking that it is service to God has become rampant in our days. A heart without God is desperately wicked. It is only by the Holy Spirit that love of God is poured abroad in our hearts! Let your heart be yielded to God and you will operate from a place of love and compassion.

Points to Ponder

1. Are you willing to be gathered together by Jesus?
2. Is there anything keeping you from going to Him with every desire, hope, and prayer?

KINDLY CRUEL

*And even as **they did not like to retain God in their knowledge,** God gave them over to a debased mind, to do those things which are not fitting; being filled with all unrighteousness, sexual immorality, wickedness, covetousness, maliciousness; full of envy, murder, strife, deceit, evil-mindedness; they are whisperers, backbiters, haters of God, violent, proud, boasters, inventors of evil things, disobedient to parents, undiscerning, untrustworthy, unloving, unforgiving, unmerciful* (Romans 1:28-31).

INDEED, as the Bible says be aware that *"**the kindest acts** of the wicked **are cruel**"* (Prov. 12:10b). Don't be deceived—those without God may appear to be kind, but often it is only for a season. When the circumstance demands, they default to their debased nature—wickedness. Of such people be careful, but continue to pray for them.

Points to Ponder

1. Do you know people who seem to be friendly and nice yet are filled with all unrighteousness?
2. What should be your response to people who offer kindness but your spirit tells you otherwise?

Reading the Bible in a Year: Genesis 18-19 and Matthew 6.

DIFFERENT TYPES OF PEOPLE

*The people **stood watching,** and the rulers even sneered at him. They said, "He saved others; let him save himself if he is God's Messiah, the Chosen One." The **soldiers** also came up and **mocked him.** They offered him wine vinegar and said, "If you are the king of the Jews, save yourself." There was a written notice above him, which read: THIS IS THE KING OF THE JEWS. One of the **criminals** who hung there **hurled insults** at him: "Aren't you the Messiah? Save yourself and us!" But the other criminal rebuked him. "Don't you fear God," he said, "since you are under the same sentence? We are punished justly, for we are getting what our deeds deserve. But this man has done nothing wrong." Then he said, "Jesus, **remember me** when you come into your kingdom (Luke 23:35-42).*

D IFFERENT types of people in the world are symbolized in the different reactions of the people who witnessed His crucifixion. Those who stood watching are easily swayed by crowd mentality, those who prefer to stand by doing nothing. The soldiers who mocked Him abused their privileged positions. The criminal hanging nearby who insulted Him represents people who come close yet still miss the opportunity of knowing Him as Lord and Savior. The other criminal who said, *"Jesus remember me,"* represents those who receive Him. It is never too late to accept Him as your Savior! The choice is yours!

Point to Ponder

1. Which type are you?

_____

_____

APPOINTMENT WITH DESTINY

Now he [Jesus] **had to** *go through Samaria* (John 4:4).

YOUR appointment with destiny is often a symphony of divine events. People, places, time, and circumstances all play parts in meeting your divine appointments. On His way to Galilee, Jesus came to Jacob's well. His disciples *had to* be away at the time. The Samaritan woman *had to* draw water, and so she came to Jacob's well. She *had to* meet Jesus. *Had* any of these not taken place, she might not have met Him when she did. The rest of the story is history! For her, this symphony of events changed her life. For you, on the day of your divine appointment, may people places, time, and circumstances line up with the will of God for you.

Points to Ponder

1. Have you ever been pleasantly surprised at how seemingly impossible plans all fell into place at the right time?

2. Have you enjoyed a symphony of events that led to your appointment with destiny?

THE FEAST OF ESTHER

...Esther...obtained grace and favor in his sight more than all the virgins. ...Then the king made a great feast, the Feast of Esther... (Esther 2:17-18 NKJV).

ESTHER was so blessed that a national feast was named after her. On the way to this exalted place, Esther taught us a valuable lesson. Sacrifice! Sacrifice is the giving up of something for what is considered more valuable. When her people were threatened, Esther called a fast in the palace and in the community. She was ready to do what nobody else has ever done before, approach the king without his invitation. She said "If I perish, I perish." She didn't perish and instead saved her people and earned the Esther Feast! Your sacrifice will speak for and lead you to your own eternal feast with Him.

Points to Ponder

1. Have you obtained grace and favor in God's sight by loving Him with all your heart, and mind, and soul?

2. Do you know that He is waiting for you right now to ask Him into your life?

3. Are you ready to sit down and feast with your heavenly Father?

THE CURSE ON YOUR PROSPERITY IS BROKEN

*And being in agony, He prayed more earnestly. Then His sweat became like great drops of blood **falling down to the ground*** (Luke 22:44 NKJV).

FOLLOWING Adam's sin, God cursed the prosperity of the ground. Genesis 3:17 says, *"Cursed is the ground because of you; through painful toil you will eat food of it"*—a curse directed to the ground the source of livelihood for the earth and all the earth creatures. God cursed the ground even further: *"By the sweat of your brow you will eat your food"* (Gen. 3:19). But **Jesus broke this curse** for you and for me. His blood instead of our blood, His sweat instead of our sweat fell on the ground satisfying that pronounced curse that stood against Adam's descendants for those who believe!

Points to Ponder

1. Have you accepted this truth that the curse on your prosperity is broken?
2. Are you trying to handle financial issues without His help?
3. Pray for faith in His promises.

January 12

THE CURSE IS REVERSED!

*The thief does not come except to steal, and to kill, and to destroy. I have come that they may have **life,** and that they may have it **more abundantly*** (John 10:10 NKJV).

JESUS reversed the curse and turned it into life abundantly! He came that you would have life and have it more abundantly; no more painful toil; no more endless misery or sweat of agony. This life is only available to those who receive and believe in Him. The choices are yours: choose life instead of death, choose success instead of failure, choose prosperity instead of endless toil and the misery of lack. Please choose Jesus!

Points to Ponder

1. Are you toiling needlessly?
2. Are you making wise, godly choices?

YOU CANNOT BE STOPPED

It is the Lord that advanced Moses and Aaron...
(1 Samuel 12:6 KJV).

WHEN God advances you, no one can stop you! Moses and Aaron led the Israelites out of Egypt. They led the people through the difficult terrain of the desert. The odds were against them in many ways and the people often turned their anger on them. In all of this, though, Moses and Aaron held on to their divine assignment—God was with them helping and advancing them against all odds. Pray the Lord will bring you advancement. Pray that God will break the spirit of delay in your life. I believe that this is what He is saying right now over your life: *"None of my words will be delayed any longer; whatever I say will be fulfilled, declares the Sovereign Lord"* (Ezekiel 12:28).

Points to Ponder

1. Does it seem as if all the odds are against you?
2. Your marriage?
3. Your job?
4. Your relationship with your children?

God will advance His perfect plan for you—pray to Him, trust His answer.

_____

_____

_____

GOD HAS COME TO HELP HIS PEOPLE

God has come to help his people (Luke 7:16b).

AFTER Jesus raised from death the only son of the widow of Nain, the people made this remarkable statement: *"God has come to help his people"* (Luke 7:16b). I am sure they said this because what they saw was beyond what mere mortal man can do. They knew that the supernatural realm touched humanity. And they were right. May you come to the realization that God has now come to help you! May God's wisdom have results *(children)* in your life, just as the Bible says, *"But wisdom is proved right by all her children"* (Luke 7:35). Also *good success* is one of *her children,* and that too is coming to you.

Points to Ponder

1. Do you believe that God has come to help you?
2. Do you lean on God's promises in His word?
3. Do you seek wisdom from the Holy Spirit within you?

MY HELP COMES FROM THE LORD

I lift up my eyes to the mountains—where does my help come from? My help comes from the Lord, the Maker of heaven and earth (Psalm 121:1-2).

THE mountain could be so big that it is hard not to notice its prominence. As imposing as mountains can sometimes be, remember that true help always come from God, not from the high and exalted worldly places or people. The psalmist says though the mountain may engage his focus, he is confident that his help is from God! Every flesh will fail, but God never fails. I pray that God will send you help from His sanctuary: *"May he [God] send you help from the sanctuary and grant you support from Zion"* (Ps. 20:2).

Points to Ponder

1. Are you too proud to ask for help from God?
2. Do your problems loom like mountains before you?
3. What keeps you from trusting Him completely to help you in every circumstance?

GOD WILL VALIDATE YOU

*The staff belonging to the man I choose will sprout, and I
will rid myself of this constant grumbling against you by the
Israelites* (Numbers 17:5).

THE budding of Aaron's staff was so God could validate Aaron
as the chosen one. Like Aaron and Moses, sometimes in life we
come across situations that may tend to trip us off our course. But
hold on! God came to the rescue of Aaron and Moses—and He will
for you also. What He does for one He can do for another. In the
process of Aaron's validation, God brought life out a dead situation
to make His point! Pray that the Lord will bring life out of dead situations
to vindicate and validate you.

Points to Ponder

1. Are you in need of God's validation?
2. Are you hoping that God will vindicate you?
3. Have you prayed about it?

THE NEED FOR CONSTANT PRAYER

*Then Jesus told his disciples a parable to show them that they
should always pray and not give up (Luke 18:1).*

P RAYERS connect us with the power of God. We should never go
on holiday from prayers. In fact, the passage also went on further
to admonish us that we ought to always pray and faint not. Constant
prayer is key if you are to match the realities of your life with the
promises of God to you!

Point to Ponder

1. Can your prayer life be improved? List a few ways you
    can bring your prayer life up to the next level.

UNTIL THE ANSWER COMES

*One day Jesus told His disciples a story to illustrate **their need for constant prayer** and to show them that they must **keep praying until the answer comes*** (Luke 18:1 Living Bible).

THIS verse in Luke 18 is from the Living Bible's translation of what Jesus told His disciples. Indeed it is a cardinal truth of life. A prayerful person is a powerful person. Never give up on prayers, sooner or later your answer will come. Jesus Christ also told them another story and concluded, *"For the proud shall be humbled but the humble shall be honored"* (Luke 1:14b Living Bible). Failure to pray is a sign of pride.

Points to Ponder

1. Do you agree that failure to pray is a sign of pride?
2. Why don't you pray more often?
3. How often is "often enough" to pray?

_____

_____

_____

WHEN YOU SEEK GOD, YOU WILL FIND HIM

"You will seek me and find me when you seek me with all your heart. I will be found by you," declares the Lord, "and will bring you back from captivity. I will gather you from all the nations and places where I have banished you," declares the Lord, "and will bring you back to the place from which I carried you into exile" (Jeremiah 29:13-14).

GOD is never far away from His people. He knows our every thought, movement, pain, and joy. May you experience Him in areas you have not known him before.

Points to Ponder

1. Have you taken the time lately to seek God with all your heart?

2. Do you believe He can be found?

THE BOOKS OF GOD

*He replied, "Do you know why I have come? I am here to tell you what is written in the **Book of the Future**. Then, when I leave, I will go again to fight my way back, past the prince of Persia; and after him, the prince of Greece. Only Michael, the angel who guards your people Israel, will be there to help me"*
(Daniel 10:20-21 Living Bible).

THERE are many books in heaven. The Bible speaks of the Book of Life, the book of remembrance, the book of the wars of the Lord, the Book of the Future, to name a few. God gave one book to Apostle John—the book of Revelation! Have you read it? It is the book of the future church. God gave books to Moses: Genesis, Exodus, Leviticus, and Deuteronomy. Have you read them? Jesus came in the volume of the books.

At any time, whether you know or it or not, you are either reading or writing a book from the Lord. Posterity will read the book of your life written or unwritten. Please make sure your story is a good book of the Lord; because when tomorrow comes, people will read it whether you like it or not.

Points to Ponder

1. Have you ever considered the book God is writing about you?

2. Are you going to be happy with its contents?

THE ARMOR OF HIS WORD

Every day he [Jesus Christ] *was teaching at the temple. But the chief priests, the teachers of the law and the leaders among the people were trying to kill him. Yet they could not find any way to do it, because all the people hung on his words* (Luke 19:47-48).

THE religious leaders heard about Him; but when He came, they could not recognize Him as the Son of God. So in their ignorance they sought to kill Him. However, in His humanity, Jesus was protected by the word of God. As you leave home today, take the word with you! God sustains *"all things by his powerful word"* (Heb. 1:3).

Point to Ponder

1. The more of the word you have within your heart, mind, and spirit, the more protection surrounds you. Jesus used the word when the enemy tried to tempt Him— can you do the same?

THE BATTLE BELONGS TO GOD

All those gathered here will know that it is not by sword or spear that the Lord saves; for the battle is the Lord's... (1 Samuel 17:47).

THE verse above is what David said to Goliath. To put it simply, the odds were against David, but the Lord fought for him and for Israel. Whatever may be standing in your way today, be assured, God will fight for you! It is never about the intensity of the battle—it has always been about God and how His people relate to Him. For instance, consider the man mentioned in Psalm 34:6 (NKJV), *"This poor man cried out, and the Lord heard him and saved him out of **all** his troubles."* God delivered the man not from most of troubles but *all* his troubles because he cried out to Him. Our God will deliver you from all your troubles.

Points to Ponder

1. Are you willing to let God fight your battles?
2. Are you assured of His victory on your behalf?
3. Have you cried out to him lately?

Reading the Bible in a Year: Exodus 1-3 and Matthew 15:21-39.

FOR YOUR DELIVERANCE

*for I know that through your prayers and God's provision of
the Spirit of Jesus Christ what has happened to me will turn
out for my deliverance* (Philippians 1:19).

WHATEVER you may be going through, it will turn out for your
good, for your deliverance. On your part, there is at least
something you can do; decree justice to every injustice in your life
no matter what is confronting you. As the Bible says, you too can
ask God to, *"Arise, Lord in your anger; rise up against the rage of my
enemies. Awake, my God; decree justice"* (Ps. 7:6). May the Lord exalt
your head *above the enemies who surround* you and may you make
music to the Lord, and may you fulfill your heavenly assignment on
earth. In the end, you will have cause to say like Paul said, *"I was not
disobedient to the heavenly vision"* (Acts 26:19).

Points to Ponder

1. Have you experienced injustice?
2. What was your reaction?
3. Did you take the issue to God in prayer?

RESTORATION IS COMING

The desert and the parched land will be glad; the wilderness **will rejoice** *and blossom. Like the crocus, it* **will burst** *into bloom; it will rejoice greatly and shout for joy. The glory of Lebanon* **will be** *given to it, the splendor of Carmel and Sharon; they* **will see** *the glory of the Lord, the splendour of our God. Strengthen the feeble hands, steady the knees that give way; say to those with fearful hearts, "Be strong, do not fear; your* **God will come**, *he will come with vengeance; with divine retribution he* **will come to save** *you"* (Isaiah 35:1-4).

PICTURE this, the prophet Isaiah speaks of a coming time when restoration will come from many angles! Glory and excellence shall be restored to you. Be patient, strong, and unafraid.

Points to Ponder

1. Are you looking forward to the time when the parched land of your spirit will be glad again?

2. Can you rejoice and blossom while waiting to see God's glory in your life?

3. Can you be strong and not fearful?

GOD IS A FINISHER

Would I ever bring this nation to the point of birth and then not deliver it?" asks the Lord. "No! I would never keep this nation from being born," says your God (Isaiah 66:9 NLT).

OUR God is the finisher of our faith—the salvation of every nation. You can rest assured that He will complete what He started in your life. Your blessings are nearer than you think. I believe that God, *"thwarts the plans of the crafty, so that their hands achieve no success"* (Job 5:12)—and He will do so in your life. And, *"Likewise, whatever the Lord our God has given us, we will possess"* (Judg. 11:24b).

Points to Ponder

1. Can you imagine all the blessings that God is waiting to give you?
2. Are you ready to possess his gifts?
3. Do you believe that He will finish His good work in you?

GOD IS ON YOUR SIDE

Who will rise up for me against the wicked? Who will take a stand for me against evildoers? Unless the Lord had given me help, I would soon have dwelt in the silence of death. When I said, "My foot is slipping," **your unfailing love, Lord, supported me** *(Psalm 94:16-18).*

LET this passage emboldened you, whatever may surround you. Stand for righteousness whether in secret or in the public. And know that if God be for you, who can be against you? Stand with the psalmist who knew that, *"Unless the Lord had given me help, I would soon have dwelt in silence of death."* You can overcome anything and anyone when you place your trust and faith in the Lord.

Points to Ponder

1. Do you have wicked people knocking at your door?
2. Are there evildoers rapping at the window?
3. Does it seem as if your foot is slipping and you are about to lose your balance? The Lord will support you—believe it!

MEDITATE ON THIS

You, O Lord, keep my lamp burning; my **God turns my darkness into light***. It is God who* **arms me with strength** *and makes my way perfect. He makes my feet like the feet of a deer, He causes [enables] me to stand on the heights. He trains my hands for battle, my arms can bend a bow of bronze. You make* **your saving help my shield, and your right hand sustains me; your help has made me great** (Psalm 18:28,32-35).

L ET these promises from Psalm 18 be realities in your life. One way this can happen is to come to the realization that when you spend time *on* God and *with* God, you make room for God's peace and His power. Always remember this! May this be your testimony.

Points to Ponder

1. When is the last time God turned your darkness into light?

2. Do you feel stronger after spending time in His word?

3. Do you use your salvation as your shield?

BITING THE HAND THAT FEEDS YOU

How much more severely do you think someone deserves to be punished who has trampled the Son of God underfoot, who has treated as an unholy thing the blood of the covenant that sanctified them, and who has insulted the Spirit of grace?
(Hebrews 10:29)

I T comes down to biting the hand that feeds you! Whenever we trample on the grace of God by which we were redeemed, we insult the Son of God. If we fail to treat others as He has treated us, we are biting the finger of Christ!

Points to Ponder

1. Have you consistently treated others with the love of Christ?

2. Have you ever considered the possibility that you may have insulted the Spirit of grace?

3. In what ways may you have unintentionally "trampled the Son of God underfoot"?

SEASON OF REPENTANCE

A broken and a contrite heart, O God, you will not ignore
(Psalm 51:17 Living Bible).

KNOWING that God will not ignore a broken and contrite heart is why we should continue to repent for the land, the people, and for ourselves. *"Don't keep looking at my sins—erase them from your sight. Create in me a new, clean heart, O God, filled with clean thoughts and right desires. A broken and a contrite heart O God, you will not ignore"* (Psalm 51:9-10,17 Living Bible). Truly, if we say we have no sin, the truth is not in us! If that is the case, we ought to live a life of continuous repentance so we find God's grace in times of need. Say a prayer of repentance today and do something or show the fruit of repentance.

Points to Ponder

1. Have you set your heart to be broken and contrite?
2. What does contrite mean to you?
3. Can you accept that only God can mend your broken heart?

OUR GREAT COMMISSION

[Jesus said] *I pray for them. I am **not praying for the world,** but for those you have given me, **for they are yours*** (John 17:9).

THIS verse from John is startling. Apparently there were some people Jesus did not pray for. He commissioned us, *"Go into all the world and preach the good news to all creation. Whoever believes... will be saved"* (Mark 16:15-16). Therefore He has left it to us to pray for these people!

Points to Ponder

1. Do you regularly pray for others?
2. Are your prayers mostly about your wants and needs?
3. What do these two verses in Mark 16 mean to you?

PRAY FOR THE WORLD'S UNSAVED

but because Jesus lives forever, he has a permanent priesthood.
Therefore he is able to save completely those who come to God
*through him, **because he always lives to intercede for them***
(Hebrews 7:24-25).

WHEN we share the gospel with others and they become saved, they are counted among those the Lord prays for. Therefore, it is our duty to pray for the unsaved in the world; this is the duty of humankind! Truly we can say to all who will listen, *"Salvation is found in no one else, for there is no other name under heaven given to mankind by which we must be saved"* (Acts 4:12). The Lord is a good God.

Points to Ponder

1. How comfortable are you sharing your testimony with others?

2. Have you told your family about the good news of the gospel?

3. Your co-workers?

4. Your neighbors?

GREAT LIGHT AND
GREAT JOY FOR ALL PEOPLE

*The people walking in darkness have seen a **great light;** on those living in the land of deep darkness a light has dawned*
(Isaiah 9:2).

THE angel said to the shepherds, *"I bring you good news that will cause **great joy** for all the people"* (Luke 2:10b). This therefore is the day that the Lord has made! On your part, defeat the cold weather; brave the wind, the truth remains that wise people still seek Jesus (see Matt. 2:1-2).

Points to Ponder

1. Do you have great joy in every part of your life, or are there pockets of darkness?

2. What can you do to shed God great light into those areas of your life?

BUILD UP YOUR CONFIDENCE— NO MATTER WHAT

*So **do not throw away your confidence;** it will be richly rewarded. You need to persevere so that when you have done the will of God, you will receive what he has promised. For in just a very little while he who is coming will come and will not delay* (Hebrews 10:35-37).

THE Bible says that at a very critical time in David's life, when it appears that everything meaningful around him collapsed that David encouraged himself in the Lord. The Lord is our ever-present help in times of need. There is one thing the devil or life situations cannot take from you—your right to choose Today, determine to encourage yourself.

Points to Ponder

1. Are you easily discouraged?
2. Are you in the habit of throwing pity parties?
3. How often do you toss away your confidence?

KEEP HOPE ALIVE

Therefore we do not lose heart. Though outwardly we are wasting away, yet inwardly we are being renewed day by day (2 Corinthians 4:16).

LET your inward grace outshine your outward struggles. Let every circumstance that may come your way be instruments that sharpen your spirit for more Christ-likeness!

Points to Ponder

1. Are you willing to allow God to turn your struggles into joys?
2. Can you see your current challenges as future character builders?

_____

_____

_____

THE RIGHTEOUS LIVE BY FAITH

But my righteous one will live by faith. And I take no pleasure in the one who shrinks back. But we do not belong to those who shrink back and are destroyed, but to those who have faith and are saved (Hebrews 10:38-39).

O UR hope is in Christ Jesus; He is our substance of things not seen. Because He died and rose again, we can face tomorrow. Without faith, it is impossible to please God! Faith is our spiritual weapon to fight the good fight.

Points to Ponder

1. Do you ever feel like shrinking back—from God, from church, from work, from relationships?

2. Why do you think you feel that way?

3. What can you do—what have you done—to eliminate that feeling?

CROSSING YOUR JORDAN

When it [the ark of the covenant] *crossed the Jordan, the waters of the Jordan were cut off. These stones are to be a memorial to the people of Israel forever* (Joshua 4:7).

AS the Lord safely brought the ark and His people across the Jordan, so He will do for you. The stones were a memorial to the people of Israel forever. God established Joshua in the presence of the Jews, so will God approve and establish you in the midst of your people.

Points to Ponder

1. Can you walk confidently through raging waters knowing that God will provide a way out?

2. Are there markers in your life that cause you to remember His mercy and grace?

GIANT-KILLING STONES

*Then he took his staff in his hand, chose five smooth stones
from the stream, put them in the pouch of his shepherd's bag
and, with his sling in his hand, approached the Philistine*
(1 Samuel 17:49-50).

UNLIKE the remembrance stones placed after crossing the Jordan, David gathered stones from a brook in preparation to kill Goliath. Have you ever wondered why David took five smooth stones but used only one to kill Goliath (see 1 Sam. 17:49-50)? I think he may have wanted to be prepared just in case Goliath's brothers showed up! I believe David's anointing is coming upon you, and that you have four giant-killing stones at your disposal. They are waiting for you in the spiritual realm and you can use them in the natural realm any time. You can kill any giant that may come across your path in life—you have the anointing! Remember the Son of David— Jesus Christ—triumphed over the enemy, and you are seated with Him in heavenly places (see Eph. 2:6).

Points to Ponder

1. Are you facing a giant?
2. Have you readied your supernatural slingshot to hold the stones that David reserved for you?
3. Do you have the courage to destroy the giant?

JOYOUS VICTORY

*May we shout for joy over your victory and lift up our banners
in the name of our God. May the Lord grant all your requests*
(Psalm 20:5).

THIS is the kind of people God is looking for as the Bible admonishes us to rejoice with those who rejoice and encourage each other with spiritual songs. When we pray for others, we activate our dormant promises; and when we rejoice with others, we facilitate Heaven's agenda on earth for our lives. The Lord indeed is our teacher! Be blessed by the words of the psalmist in Psalm 20:5. Indeed, when you rejoice with those who rejoice, your victory will move closer than you can ever imagine.

Points to Ponder

1. Are you happy when others succeed, or does the enemy slip a bit of envy into your thoughts?

2. How easy is it for you to shout for joy over another person's victory?

A Season of Reward

And my honesty will testify for me in the future
(Genesis 30:33a).

YOU have come to a season of reward. Your honesty, labors of love, and your goodness and righteousness toward others will speak for you—to God and to those around you. Anytime you choose to do right, people will notice and you will earn yourself a season of reward. As God remembered Noah (see Gen. 8:1), He will remember you and your good works. The Lord will remember you and break any limitation around you if you strive to fulfill His will for your life. *"The **seed will grow** well, the vine will **yield its fruit,** the **ground will produce** its crops, and **the heavens will drop their dew.** I will **give all these things** as an inheritance to the remnant of this people"* (Zech. 8:12).

Points to Ponder

1. Are you an honest person?
2. Do you bend the truth depending on who you are talking to?
3. Do you see yourself as righteous?

GREAT THINGS HAPPEN TO BELIEVERS

*Then Jesus declared, "I am the bread of life. Whoever comes to me will **never go hungry,** and whoever believes in me will **never be thirsty** (John 6:35).*

I F you believe in God and Jesus, the Son of God, nothing shall be impossible. Great things happen for those who believe! Here are some of these great things:

1. You will behold the glory of God (see John 11:40).
2. You will see Heaven open and angels (see John 1:50-51).
3. Your prayers will be answered (see Matt. 21:22).
4. You will never go hungry or be thirsty (see John 6:35).
5. You will be healed (see Matt. 9:28-30).

Points to Ponder

1. As a believer, does your personal testimony prove that great things actually do happen to those who believe?
2. Write your testimony here, then share it with everyone God leads you to.

THE SPIRIT GIVES LIFE

*The Spirit gives life; the flesh counts for nothing. The words I
have spoken to you—they are full of the Spirit and life*
(John 6:63).

THE essence of life on earth came from the Spirit of God and is sustained by the Spirit and the word of God. God spoke creation into being and the moral ground is framed by the word we speak. Speak life always, speak out of your spirit because your flesh profits nothing.

Points to Ponder

1. What does it mean that the flesh counts for nothing?
2. Do you more often speak from your spirit or your flesh?

BEWARE OF STRANGE DOCTRINE

Do not be carried away by all kinds of strange teachings. It is good for our hearts to be strengthened by grace, not by eating ceremonial foods, which is of no benefit to those who do so (Hebrews 13:9).

STRANGE teachings, or doctrines, are often melodramatic phi-losophy or dramatic manifestations that are contrary to the teachings of God. Often they may seem relevant, but are in reality empty and bear no tangible relevance to the essence of a godly life. Keep your mind and thoughts on Jesus Christ and His crucifixion! He is the Author and Finisher of our faith.

Points to Ponder

1. Have you ever been carried away or subtly influences by false or strange teachings?
2. Maybe by false prophets or healers?

SPIRITUAL DRIFT

We must pay the most careful attention, therefore, to what we have heard, so that we do not drift away (Hebrews 2:1).

SPIRITUAL drifting is a gradual erosion of values and failing to do for God what we used to do. The drifting can be very subtle and commonly imperceptible, but like a worm it eats from within. The problem of spiritual drifting from the core values of Christianity may not be as rare as many think. We all drift at one time or the other; but it is important to reverse the drift after realizing the change. We need to stop, reflect, take heed despite the busyness of our routines. When you sense drifting spiritually, you must listen to God's word, look at the signs that confirm the message, and then stop to assess why you are drifting and return to God. The palmist says, *"One thing I ask from the LORD, this only do I seek: that I may dwell in the house of the Lord all the days of my life"* (Ps. 24:4).

Points to Ponder

1. Are you guilty of spiritually drifting away from God and His destiny for you?

2. Have you recently taken time to evaluate where you are spiritually in your walk with Him?

_____

_____

_____

THE FATE OF THE WICKED

A worthless person, a wicked man, walks with a perverse mouth; he winks with his eyes, he shuffles his feet, he points with his fingers; perversity is in his heart, he devises evil continually, he sows discord. Therefore his calamity shall come suddenly; suddenly he shall be broken without remedy
(Proverbs 6:12-15 NKJV).

NEVER envy the wicked; their reign, if any, is always short lived! The wicked are on slippery slopes and unless they repent will surely be destroyed. That is why the Living Bible says, *"Let me describe for you a worthless and a wicked man; first, he is a constant liar; he signals his true intentions to his friends with eyes and feet and fingers. Next, his heart is full of rebellion. And he spends his time thinking of all the evil he can do, and stirring up discontent. But **he will be destroyed suddenly, broken beyond hope of healing**"* (Proverbs 6:12-15). Goodness will never fail. Do something good, and in due season it will speak out for you.

Points to Ponder

1. Do you know a wicked person?
2. Have you witnessed his or her downfall?
3. If not, do you believe that downfall is imminent for the wicked?

THE FUTURE OF A GOOD PERSON

*Blessed is the one who does not walk in step with the wicked
or stand in the way that sinners take or sit in the
company of mockers (Psalm 1:1).*

THE future of good people is bright! *"The good man walks along
in the ever-brightening light of God's favor; the dawn gives way
to morning splendor! While the evil man gropes and stumbles in the
dark"* (Prov. 4:18-19 Living Bible). So today, let your light so shine
that people will glorify your God. *"Not so the wicked! They are like
chaff that the wind blows away. Therefore the wicked will not stand
in the judgment, nor sinners in the assembly of the righteous. For the
LORD watches over the way of the righteous, but the way of the wicked
leads to destruction"* (Ps. 1:4-6).

Points to Ponder

1. Are you known by others as a good person?
2. Why or why not?

RESIST THE DEVIL

So let God work his will in you. Yell a loud no to the Devil and watch him scamper. Say a quiet yes to God and he'll be there in no time. Quit dabbling in sin. Purify your inner life. Quit playing the field. Hit bottom, and cry your eyes out. The fun and games are over. Get serious, really serious. Get down on your knees before the Master; it's the only way you'll get on your feet (James 4:7 The Message).

THE more traditional version of this verse is in the New King James, which says, *"Therefore submit to God. Resist the devil and he will flee from you"* (James 4:7). Remember too that *"God raised us up with Christ and seated us with him in the heavenly realms in Christ Jesus"* (Eph. 2:6)—far above all principalities and evil powers. Once you take your stand against evil, you draw nearer to God; and in turn God draws you even closer to Himself and puts you in the shadow of His glorious presence! That is where you want to be, protected and secure in Him.

Points to Ponder

1. Have you yelled a loud NO to the devil lately?
2. Have you said a quiet yes to God lately?
3. How about getting on your knees so that you can get back up on your feet?

TIME TO ADVANCE

You have made your way around this hill country long enough; now turn north. You have stayed long enough at this mountain. Break camp and advance into the hill country...
(Deuteronomy 1:6-7 Living Bible).

T HIS is a good word for you today. Endless circling and unnecessary repetition is cancelled in your life. You are not to waste one more day doing the same things that bring no advancement! Enough is enough, and you have suffered enough. You will break out of the monotony of an endless circle of failure. Burst out into bloom like the crocus. Divine advancement is come upon you!

Points to Ponder

1. Is it easier for you to stay in a comfortable yet unproductive condition than to break camp and advance?

2. Are you fearful?

BEGIN TO TAKE POSSESSION!

*"See, I have given into your hand Sihon the Amorite, king of Heshbon, and his country. **Begin to take possession** of it and engage him in battle." The Lord said to me, "See, I have begun to deliver Sihon and his country over to you. Now **begin to conquer and possess** his land"* (Deuteronomy 2:24,31).

CONTENTMENT with godliness is a great reward! God is able to prompt you and nudge you into action—and even more if you are standing right with Him and your ways are pleasing to Him. When God leads, He expects you to follow. He will tell you when to fight or hold your peace; and as you know, by His strength you will prevail. Today God is saying that you should begin to take possession of your promises.

Points to Ponder

1.   What is your response to God's prompting and nudging?
2.   Are you excited to take action?
3.   Are you prepared to stand with and for Him?

YOUR WORDS FRAME YOUR WORLD

[Jesus said] *The words I have spoken to you—they are full of the spirit and life* (John 6:63).

M ANY people are today experiencing the fruit of the words they spoke yesterday. Words have the power of life and death, words can make and unmake. So much so that the Son of God came as *The Word!* There is a strong connection between the spoken word and the spirit realm. Repent for the negative words of yesterday and today speak the word of life to situations around you!

Points to Ponder

1. How many times have you spoken words that tear down rather than build up?
2. How hard is it for you to bridle your tongue?
3. What steps can you take to say only those things that are godly and uplifting—for yourself and others to hear?

NOT IN VAIN

Unless the Lord builds the house, the builders labor in vain.
Unless the Lord watches over the city, the guards stand watch
in vain (Psalm 127:1).

UNLESS the Lord builds your house, you are laboring in vain. This is my prayer for you, that you will realize how much God love and cares for your family whether they are far or near. Allow God to build your home, your relationships, and your career, and your heart.

Points to Ponder

1. Are you working to no avail?
2. Are you single-handedly striving to build your own house rather than allowing God to build your home?

OPEN DOOR OF OPPORTUNITY

*a great door for effective work has opened to me, and there
are many who oppose me* (1 Corinthians 16:9).

THERE is a great and effective door opened to you—to all those
who love the Lord. Some time ago, it came to me like a mighty
rushing wind, but today I think this word is for *you!* Ignore whatever
oppositions confront you; a great opening, opportunity, has come for
you. Your present challenge is an indication that it is time to move
up. May the Lord break the spirit of stagnation and delay and may
divine acceleration come upon you!

Points to Ponder

1. As you read the verse and message for you, did an
   opportunity come to mind?

2. Are you willing to step out into an effective work for the
   Lord?

_____

_____

_____

"Go and Tell" Seasons

*Then the word of the Lord came to Isaiah: "**Go and tell**
Hezekiah, 'This is what the Lord, the God of your father
David, says: I have heard your prayer and seen your tears; I
will add fifteen years to your life. And I will deliver you and
this city from the hand of the king of Assyria. I will defend this
city* (Isaiah 38:4-6).

THE "go and tell" season is the season when you boast on God
and His ways. Such seasons were common in Bible days: King
Hezekiah was on his sick bed and received the word he would not
survive his illness, but he prayed and God added fifteen years to his
life. God instructed Isaiah to "go and tell" King Hezekiah he would
receive healing. This is the season to tell you that your healing has
come.

Points to Ponder

1. Is there something God wants you to go and tell?
2. Have you gone?
3. Has God instructed someone to tell you something He
    wants you to know?
4. Have you listened?

"GO AND TELL" SEASONS
CONTINUED

*As Obadiah was walking along, Elijah met him. Obadiah recognized him, bowed down to the ground, and said, "Is it really you, my lord Elijah?" "Yes," he replied. "**Go tell** your master, 'Elijah is here'"* (1 Kings 18:7-8).

E LIJAH is in town and we can hear the sound of abundance of rain; the famine has ended. Yes, there are times we need to challenge our situation with the promises of God in our lives and with the testimonies of our past experiences rather than allow the situation to challenge our promises! The seasons have changed in our favor, and now go and tell Ahab the famine will not last forever because God has promised an abundance of rain.

Points to Ponder

1. Can you believe for things that are not visible at the moment?

2. Can you believe for that healing, job, mended relationship?

3. Hope in God—He is ever faithful.

"Go and Tell" Seasons
Continued

[Isaiah spoke of and foretold Cyrus] *This is what the Lord says to his anointed, to Cyrus, whose right hand I take hold of to subdue nations before him and to strip kings of their armor, to open doors before him so that gates will not be shut* (Isaiah 45:1).

THE Lord has opened double doors before us, evil kings have been stripped of their armor and the gates of blessings will no longer be shut to us. Yes, indeed, that is why the Bible says the Breaker Himself has gone ahead of us and the Breaker's anointing (see Micah 2:13) is upon us!

Points to Ponder

1. Do you believe that the Lord is going before you, opening doors and gates?

2. What do you think is on the other side of those open doors and gates?

3. Are you willing to accept His blessings?

"GO AND TELL" SEASONS
CONTINUED

[Moses told Pharaoh] *Our livestock too must go with us; not a hoof is to be left behind. We have to use some of them in worshiping the Lord our God...* (Exodus 10:26).

OUR time has come; the season has changed and toil and hardship is over; slavery has ended; we are going to the Promised Land. Furthermore, we are going with all the Lord has given us, "not a hoof" will be left behind. Yes, the past is behind us, we will move forward and leave nothing to the devil; moving into the future, nothing broken and nothing missing!

Points to Ponder

1. You are complete in God. Do you feel complete?
2. Does your spiritual life total who you are?
3. Are you giving any place within to the evil one?

CANCELLED DEBTS SEASON

...the Lord's time for cancelling debts has been proclaimed
(Deuteronomy 15:2).

L ET this truth of cancelled debts come to you today in a new and fresh way! This is your year to cancel all debts and that every written code that has stood against you has now been nailed to the cross and you have triumphed over them with shouts of joy. *"There need be no poor people among you, for in the land the Lord your God is giving you to possess as your inheritance, he will **richly bless you*** (Deuteronomy 15:4).

Points to Ponder

1. Have you worked hard to pay off your financial obligations?

2. Being debt-free is a glorious freedom that sets you free not only financially but emotionally and spiritually as well. Do you agree?

MAY GOD FIGHT YOUR BATTLES

Strengthen the feeble hands, steady the knees that give way... and those the Lord has rescued will return. They will enter Zion with singing; everlasting joy will crown their heads. Gladness and joy will overtake them, and sorrow and sighing will flee away (Isaiah 35:3,10).

GOD will strengthen you wherever you may be weak and gladness and joy will overtake you with His mercy and grace. Great things will grow by themselves for you, your family, your church, and your city (see Isa. 37:30). Don't think it too hard for God to do. He is the Finisher of our faith.

Points to Ponder

1. Are you weary of fighting the good fight?
2. Are your hands weak and your knees about to give way? Be hopeful! God is coming to rescue you!

Israel's Helper Will Help You

I will put in the desert, the cedar and the acacia, the myrtle and the olive. I will set pines in the wasteland, the fir and the cypress together, so that the people may see and know, may consider and understand, that the hand of the Lord has done this... (Isaiah 19-20).

GOD is able to this for you! He can turn the desert within you into a place of fruitfulness and life and growth. This is His sure word of promise for you. One of the reasons God will do this for you is that He wants show off His great works in your life! You have been chosen as the showpiece for His infinite goodness so that people will see, understand, take to heart and gain divine revelation. This is His sure word of promise to you today.

Points to Ponder

1. Do you feel dry and desolate inside?
2. Is your spirit parched like a desert?
3. Do you believe God can bring refreshing life and love to your body, mind, and spirit?

THE FRUITS OF GOD'S FAVOR

*This is what the Lord says: "In the time of my favor **I will answer you**, and in the day of salvation **I will help you**; **I will keep you** and will make you to be a **covenant** for the people, to **restore** the land and to **reassign** its desolate inheritances (Isaiah 49:8).*

F AVOR has fruits and they manifest as divine enablement. The followings are some of the ways His favor will be revealed in your life: He will answer you; He will help you; He will keep you close to Him; He promises to restore what you have lost; He will reassign blessings to you.

Points to Ponder

1. Are you as fruitful as you would like to be?

2. Have you accepted God's divine enablement to share your fruits and blessings with others who need to see and believe in Him?

WE ARE HIS PEOPLE

*Know that the Lord, He is God; it is He who has made us,
and not we ourselves; **we are His people** and the sheep of
His pasture* (Psalm 100:3 NKJV).

THOSE who put their trust in God shall never be put to shame
and those who wait upon the Lord shall renew their strength!
God will never fail us! You belong to an exclusive club known as the
people of God; the redeemed of the Lord, purchased by the atoning
blood of Jesus Christ. That is who we are. A chosen people, a peculiar
people called out of darkness into His marvelous light. We are also
the sheep of His pasture. As a sheep in God's pasture you shall not
want—He will lead you besides still waters.

Point to Ponder

1. Psalm 100 is full of hope and encouragement, peace and
    comfort. Have you read it prayerfully and thoughtfully
    lately?

WATCHING FOR GOD

I have posted watchmen on your walls, Jerusalem; they will never be silent day or night. You who call on the Lord, give yourselves no rest, and give him no rest til he establishes Jerusalem and makes her the praise of the earth (Isaiah 62:6-7).

M ANY are familiar with watchman watching out for the devil and his agents, but the Prophet Isaiah says watch and give God no rest until He establishes work on earth. Jesus Christ taught us to pray, "God's kingdom come on earth as it is in heaven." Our watchmen should not only watch for the enemies, they should also watch for God and His will on earth.

Points to Ponder

1. Are you watchful for God and listening for His voice?
2. Are you watchful for signs of the evil one trying to slither into your life?

GOD PROTECTS YOU

Get yourself ready! ***Stand up and say to them whatever I command you.*** *Do not be terrified by them, or I will terrify you before them. Today I have made you a fortified city, an iron pillar and a bronze wall to stand against the whole land—against the kings of Judah, its officials, its priests and the people of the land.* ***They will fight against you but will not overcome you, for I am with you and will rescue you,"***
declares the Lord (Jeremiah 1:17-19).

ALTHOUGH there are some around the world who face evil armed with guns and weapons, most of us are fighting words and ideologies. When God calls you, He will protect you against all forms of attack. Today, trust and obey that He will protect you and guide your steps!

Point to Ponder

1. Are you standing up and saying whatever God commands you to say to those who oppose His salvation message?

NEVER ALONE

*No one will be able to stand up against you all the days of your life. As I was with Moses, so I will be with you; **I will never leave you nor forsake you.** Be strong and courageous...*
(Joshua 1:5-6).

THESE were the words of God to Joshua at a critical moment of transition in his life. I believe this is what God is saying to you right now! Like Joshua, often we feel the challenges in our lives are impossible to overcome; but if God says He is with us, *no one* can be against us. Your season has come because you now have double advantage; He is with you and promises that no one can stand up against you. Be bold, and indeed be courageous.

Points to Ponder

1. Have you ever taken this Scripture passage as your own—claimed it for your life?

2. If not, do you believe taking such a step would make a positive change in the way you think, believe, live?

_____

_____

_____

SURRENDER ALL TO JESUS

...For we have no power to face this vast army that is attacking us. We do not know what to do, but our eyes are upon you (2 Chronicles 20:12).

Now, our God, hear the prayers and petitions of your servant. ...Give ear, our God, and hear; open your eyes and see the desolation of the city that bears your Name. We do not make requests of you because we are righteous, but because of your great mercy. Lord, listen! Lord, forgive! O Lord, hear and act! For your sake, my God, do not delay... (Daniel 9:17-19).

HEZEKIAH prayed a prayer of submission to God in the face of overwhelming circumstances; Daniel also prayed. In both of these instances, these great men of God experienced heart-melting circumstances, but in their dire need they surrendered all to God. God did not fail them! Indeed, when you surrender all to Jesus, God will act on your behalf as the psalmist said, *"It is time for you to act, Lord"* (Ps. 119:126).

Points to Ponder

1. Have you ever petitioned God with as much fervor as Hezekiah and Daniel?
2. Why or why not?

_____

_____

_____

ALL IS POSSIBLE WITH GOD

But Moses said, The people among whom I am are 600,000 footmen [besides all the women and children], and You have said, I will give them meat, that they may eat a whole month! Shall flocks and herds be killed to suffice them? Or shall all the fish of the sea be collected to satisfy them? The Lord said to Moses, Has the Lord's hand (His ability and power) become short (thwarted and inadequate)? You shall see now whether My word shall come to pass for you or not (Numbers 11:21-23 AMP).

WHEN Moses lost sight of the ability and power of God in face of the seemingly overwhelming situation, he wondered if God could provide for His people. God always fulfills His promises—God provided manna for Moses and the people, He does the same for you.

Points to Ponder

1. Do you ever doubt God's ability and power to sustain you?

2. Do you remember a time when you doubted and He proved Himself worthy of trust and allegiance?

Reading the Bible in a Year: Deuteronomy 1-2 and Mark 11:1-19.

YOU ARE A LIGHT IN THE DARKNESS

This is how the lampstand was made: It was made of hammered gold—from its base to its blossoms. The lampstand was made exactly like the pattern the Lord had shown Moses (Numbers 8:4).

YOU are a lampstand of God on earth. May your light never go off; may the Lord keep your light burning and may your oil never cease flowing! The lampstand was made of pure gold, meaning there is divine substance in you. It was hammered out, meaning all your past experiences have molded you and made you who you are today. The base and shaft, flower-like cups, buds and blossoms were of one piece, meaning you are now standing firm, whole, and in unity with the Spirit.

Point to Ponder

1. After reading the comparison between you and God's lampstand, are you empowered enough to let your light shine for all to see?

_____

_____

_____

"COME UP HERE"

*After this I looked, there before me was a door standing open in heaven. And the voice I had first heard speaking to me like a trumpet said, "**Come up here,** and I will show you what must take place after this" (Revelation 4:1).*

TODAY I believe God is saying to you, "Come up to a new level." If God says yes, nobody can say no! In the book of Daniel, the Bible describes a book in heaven as the book of the future (see Dan. 10:20-21 Living Bible). May the Lord open unto you this great book that you may gain divine wisdom!

Points to Ponder

1. Do you wish you could see into the future?

2. Do you consult psychics, astrologers, or soothsayers? Only God Almighty can show you the future—your destiny is written only on His heart and in His Book.

DO NOT BE TERRIFIED

Do not be terrified; do not be afraid of them. **The Lord your God, who** *is going before you,* **will fight for you,** *as he did for you in Egypt, before your very eyes, and in the wilderness. There you saw how* **the Lord your God carried you,** *as a father carries his son, all the way you went until you reached this place* (Deuteronomy 1:29-31).

HOW reassuring it is to realize that God carries you as a natural parent carries a son or daughter with tenderness and ultimate affection. And it does matter whether you are young or old. It does not matter to God; He is the Father of all. Today don't be afraid; He will be with you and fight your battles. God gives you power for victory.

Points to Ponder

1. Are you sometimes afraid, sometimes terrified?
2. What is the cause of your fearfulness?
3. Can you picture in your mind God carrying you gently through any battle?

_____

_____

_____

Prayers that Stop Storms

...I will spread out my hands in prayers to the Lord. The thunder will stop and there will be no more hail so you may know that the earth is the Lord's (Exodus 9:29).

MOSES prayed to stop the thunder and the hail. Jesus also prayed and the storm on the sea ceased. You too can pray that the storms in your life will end. This power is in every believer. You can walk in such power. Moses thought he could not fulfill God's assignment, but God reassured him and eventually he walked in this awesome power of the manifestation of God. Like Moses, I pray that today any thunder and hail in your life will cease!

Points to Ponder

1. How powerful do you feel?
2. How powerful does God want you to feel?
3. Is there a difference between the two?

SOME BLESSINGS FROM PRAYING ISAIAH 58

Shout it aloud, do not hold back. Raise your voice like a trumpet...then you will find your joy in the Lord, and I will cause you to ride in triumph on the heights of the land and to feast on the inheritance of your father Jacob. For the mouth of the Lord has spoken (Isaiah 58:1-14).

AFTER reading the whole chapter of Isaiah 58, pray that:

- The bonds of wickedness will be broken
- The cords of bondage will be untied
- Every oppression will go
- Every yoke will be broken
- Your light will break forth like the dawn
- Your healing will quickly appear
- His righteousness will go before you
- The glory of the Lord will be your rear guard.

Point to Ponder

1. Do you have a prayer ritual? Blessings come from praying through the Scriptures. Start today.

SOME MORE BLESSINGS FROM PRAYING ISAIAH 58

Shout it aloud, do not hold back. Raise your voice like a trumpet...then you will find your joy in the Lord, and I will cause you to ride in triumph on the heights of the land and to feast on the inheritance of your father Jacob. For the mouth of the Lord has spoken (Isaiah 58:1-14).

A FTER reading the whole chapter of Isaiah 58, pray that:

- The Lord will answer you
- The Lord will guide you always
- He will satisfy your needs
- He will strengthen you
- You will be a well-watered garden
- You will be a spring whose waters never fail
- You will rebuild the ancient ruins in your family and in the church
- You will find your joy in the Lord
- You will ride on the heights of the land
- You will feast on the inheritance of God

Point to Ponder

1. Have you started to pray your blessings through the Scriptures? Today is a good time to start.

_____

_____

BLOOM LIKE THE CROCUS

*The desert and the parched land will be glad; the wilderness will rejoice and blossom. Like the crocus, it will **burst into bloom**... (Isaiah 35:1-2).*

THE crocus really do burst into bloom in their due season—so may the Lord cause you to burst out into bloom even in the midst of all that surrounds you. This is my prayer for you today. Also, may God be your *"sure foundation for your times"* (Isa. 33:6).

Points to Ponder

1. Do you ever feel as if you are going to burst—with stress, with worry, with heartache?

2. God wants you to burst into bloom with love, and peace, and joy. Do you believe that?

_____

_____

_____

THIS ROCK HAS WATER

"Speak to that rock before their eyes and it will pour out its water." ...Then Moses raised his arm and struck the rock twice with his staff. Water gushed out, and the community and their livestock drank" (Numbers 20:8,11).

THE Israelites saw only rocks and sand in their journey through the desert. The rock became an offense and they grumbled against Moses and God. Unknown to them even the rock of offense could be turned into what they needed the most at that time in their lives. So God said to Moses, "Speak to that rock before their eyes and it will pour out its water." Take time and look carefully at the challenges in front of you today; maybe all you need is to speak the right word!

Points to Ponder

1. Do you ever look at problems and challenges as ways to provide for your need?
2. Will you consider another perspective?

KEEP THE GRAIN AND WINE

I will never again give you to your enemies; never again shall foreign soldiers come and take away your grain and wine. You raised it; you shall keep it (Isaiah 62:8-9a Living Bible).

THIS is a great promise of God and you too can claim it as your own: God will not give you over to your enemies; others will not take the reward of your labor. This is an awesome promise; God will not allow your enemies to prevail over you. The enemy cannot overpower you. It is never about *your* strength—it is always about God's power within you!

Points to Ponder

1. Are you thankful that this promise is meant for you?
2. Have you claimed it as your own?

DIVINE CLEANSING

He [Hezekiah] did what was right in the eyes of the Lord, just as his father David had done (2 Chronicles 29:2).

AHAZ was Hezekiah's natural father, but Ahaz was an evil king and Hezekiah was a good person in sight of God. Hezekiah did well in the eyes of God, so God connected him instead to the lineage of David. His goodness and right standing with God bypassed the wickedness of his natural father and reached out to another generation to link him to the greatest king of Israel, the man after God's own heart—King David. May your life not be hindered by the sins of your bloodline. May your goodness break off any family reproach!

Points to Ponder

1. Do you sometimes feel ashamed or hindered in life because of your family's reputation?
2. Do you realize that God can give you a new lineage if you continue to do what is right in the eyes of the Lord?

Your Hard Service Is Over

Comfort, comfort my people, says your God. ...proclaim to her that hard service has been completed, that her sin has been paid for... (Isaiah 40:1-2).

YOUR days of toil and sweat are over! Now the Lord will straighten out every crooked path and smooth off the rough spots on the road for you. This blessing is yours today! Also pray Isaiah 60 into your life. Isaiah had a lot to say about the Lord and His promises and goodness.

Points to Ponder

1. Is there a difference between working to pay for your sin and working to glorify God?
2. Are you ready to walk on a path that God has straightened and smoothed for you?

_____

_____

_____

THE SOUND OF THE LORD

Hear that uproar from the city, hear that noise from the temple! It is the sound of the Lord repaying His enemies all they deserve (Isaiah 66:6).

IF you are sensitive in the spirit, you will hear His sound no matter the season. When you hear His sound, don't ignore it; God desires to speak to humankind because it is not His wish that any should perish. The prophet Isaiah said, *"Oh, that you [God] would rend the heavens and come down, that the mountains would tremble before you!"* (Isa. 64:1). Isaiah knew the sound of God and that is why he longed for it—he heard the sound and awesomeness of God's presence.

Points to Ponder

1. How sensitive is your spirit?
2. Can you slow down and open up more so that your spirit becomes more attune to the Lord's sound?
3. His voice?

Exponential Increase

...When I left home and crossed the Jordan River, I owned nothing except a walking stick. Now my household fills two large camps!" (Genesis 32:10 NLT).

May the Lord God of your fathers make you a thousand times more numerous than you are, and bless you as He has promised you (Deuteronomy 1:11 NKJV).

JACOB said that when he left home and crossed the Jordan River, he had nothing except a walking stick—then on his return, his household filled two large camps (see Gen. 32:10 NLT). And when Jacob entered Egypt, he entered as a family, but in Exodus his descendants came out of Egypt as a nation. That is exponential increase!

Points to Ponder

1. In what areas of your life would you like God to exponentially increase?

2. Do you have faith that He can—He will?

TIME TO DRAW THE LINE

"...You Levites have gone too far!" (Numbers 16:7)

H AVE you ever felt holy indignation against the devil's injustice to humankind or even man's injustice to man? Moses felt so at several points in his life, and told the Levites so in Numbers 16. It is time to tell the devil enough is enough. Why sit back and watch the devil run around with what is rightfully yours. Take back what belongs to you! The devil stirred Korah and his group to rise up against Moses; but God inspired Moses to draw the line, saying, "You Levites (Korah and group) have gone too far!" Both parties drew the line, but God won the battle—as always. Draw the line today and you will not fail!

Points to Ponder

1. Is there a situation or relationship that needs you to take a stand and draw a line?

2. Are you emboldened enough today to say, "Enough is enough!"?

LOOK AND LIVE

The Lord said to Moses, "Make a snake and put it up on a pole; anyone who is bitten can look at it and live." So Moses made a bronze snake and put it up on a pole. Then when anyone was bitten by a snake and looked at the bronze snake, they lived (Numbers 21:8-9).

WHEN the Israelites were in the wilderness, if a person was bitten by a poisonous snake and looked up to the bronze snake that hung on the pole, that person lived and did not die. This was a symbol of the pre-incarnate Jesus Christ. This Old Testament occurrence was a symbol of what was to come! Even now, whoever looks up to Jesus will be delivered from every predicament.

Points to Ponder

1. Have you ever considered this meaning of this passage in Numbers 21?
2. Do you look up to Jesus hanging on the cross as your Redeemer and Savior from all of life's predicaments?

BLOODY HATRED

Moses sent messengers from Kadesh to the king of Edom, saying: "This is what your brother Israel says: You know about all the hardships that have come upon us. Our forefathers went down into Egypt, and we lived there many years. The Egyptians mistreated us and our fathers, but when we cried out to the Lord, he heard our cry and sent an angel and brought us out of Egypt." ...Then Edom came out against them with a large and powerful army. Since Edom refused to let them go through their territory, Israel turned away from them (Numbers 20:14-21).

W HATEVER it takes, try not to allow brotherhood relationships to degenerate into hatred. If it does, often it becomes very bloody! Moses and the Israelites soon discovered that the grudge of yesterday had become an issue of bloody battle. Try and resolve issues before they deteriorate especially with your brothers; because the nearer in blood, the more bloody it could become. Know when to fight and when to retreat!

Points to Ponder

1. Do you hold a grudge against someone?
2. Does someone hold a grudge against you?
3. How important is it to God that you rectify this type of issue?

THE LORD'S BOOK OF WARS

*That is why the **Book of the Wars of the Lord** says: "...Zahab in Suphah and the ravines, the Arnon and the slopes of the ravines that lead to the settlement of Ar and lie along the border of Moab (Numbers 21:14-15).*

AS mentioned previously, there are many books in Heaven. In addition to the book of life, the book of remembrance, the Bible mentions the book of wars of the Lord! May the Lord grant you access to the books of Heaven so you can gain wisdom and knowledge about His justice and righteousness.

Points to Ponder

1. What do you think is written in the book of the wars?
2. Does it contain modern-day conflicts?
3. Is your name written there?

TWO MEN DEFEATED A POWERFUL ARMY

[Jonathan said his armor bearer] *"Perhaps the Lord will act in our behalf. Nothing can hinder the Lord from saving, whether by many or by few." Then panic struck the whole army...It was a panic sent by God. They found the Philistines in total confusion, striking each other with their swords* (1 Samuel 14:6b,15,20b).

WITH only two, God fought for Israel. Indeed, if God be for you, nobody can defeat you! God is on your side!

Points to Ponder

1. Have you teamed up with God as an army of two?
2. Do you sincerely believe that if God is for you, no one can be against you?

A NEW MEASURE OF THE SPIRIT

The Spirit of the Lord will come powerfully upon you...and you will be changed into a different person (1 Samuel 10:6).

THE angel told Mary, *"The Holy Spirit will come on you, and the power of the Most High will overshadow you"* (Luke 1:35). The impossible became possible! Samuel said to Saul that the Spirit of the Lord would come upon him powerfully. Saul had a life-transforming experience. And for Mary, she was emboldened to face the world and take on the role of Jesus' mother. May the Holy Spirit bring a new level of anointing and power to you today!

Points to Ponder

1. What does the Spirit of the Lord mean to you?
2. Can you describe Him?
3. Have you felt His power within you?

FAR FROM TROUBLE

*You'll be built solid, grounded in righteousness, far from any trouble—**nothing to fear!** far from terror—it won't even come close! If anyone attacks you, don't for a moment suppose that I sent them, and if any should attack, nothing will come of it. ...no weapon that can hurt you has ever been forged. Any accuser who takes you to court will be dismissed as a liar. This is what God's servants can expect. I'll see to it that **everything works out for the best** (Isaiah 54:11-17 The Message).*

THESE promises from God in Isaiah 54 are indeed comforting as we accept them into our hearts, minds, and spirits. As God's servants we have so very much to be thankful for.

Points to Ponder

1. Can you take the "nothing to fear" promise seriously?
2. Can you put fear to rest and be assured that God is keeping you far from terror and trouble?
3. Why or why not?

HIS PROMISES AND
YOUR PROTECTION

And Manoah said to his wife, "We shall surely die, because we have seen God!" But his wife said to him, "If the Lord had desired to kill us, He would not have accepted a burnt offering and a grain offering from our hands, nor would He have shown us all these things, nor would He have told us such things as these at this time" (Judges 13:22-23 NKJV).

THE promises of God are protective and one could say they have shields that embody protection, propelling power, and preserving force. His promises are His prophetic utterances; and because His word or prophetic promises will not return to Him void, they keep you safe against all odds until they are fulfilled. Do you have any promises yet unfilled? Like Manoah's wife said, let me say to you, you will not die before those promises are fulfilled! He has not brought you this far to abandon you or let you down! Your best days are ahead of you.

Points to Ponder

1. Do you feel safe in God's loving arms that hold you each and every moment?
2. Does His protection give you peace?

GOD IS ALWAYS NEAR

*What other nation is so great as to have their gods near them the way the **Lord our God is near us** whenever we pray to him? And what other nation is so great as to have such righteous decrees and laws as this body of laws I am setting before you today?* (Deuteronomy 4:7-8)

A S the people of God, we are privileged because the Lord is always near us. The Bible says we are great to have God always on our side. The glory of His presence is reassuring and in His presence is His righteous decrees and laws to guide us.

Points to Ponder

1. Does your nation recognize God's supreme authority?
2. Does your nation proclaim God's rightful position as a nation under God?

GOD'S SUPREMACY

Has any god ever tried to take for himself one nation out of another nation, by testings, by miraculous signs and wonders, by war, by a mighty hand and an outstretched arm, or by great and awesome deeds, like all the things the Lord your God did for you in Egypt before your very eyes? (Deuteronomy 4:34)

GOD indeed showed Himself strong on behalf of the Israelites when He took them out of Egypt. In this verse we see the various ways God can show Himself strong on your behalf: by testing—*allowing you to go through some things,* God can show His strength; by miraculous signs and wonders—*God can show supremacy* on your behalf; by wars, *demonstration of His mighty hands* and awesome deeds, God can *reveal His strength* for your case!

Points to Ponder

1. How well do you fare when God's testing comes along?
2. Are you strengthened?
3. How well do you accept miracles?
4. Are you fearful or thankful?

THE TESTING OF YOUR HEART

He gave you manna to eat in the wilderness, something your ancestors had never known, to humble and test you so that in the end it might go well with you (Deuteronomy 8:16).

THE Bible says when the people grumbled after God provided food for them. *"They whined like spoiled children, 'Why can't God give us a decent meal in this desert? Sure, he struck the rock and the water flowed, creeks cascaded from the rock. But how about some fresh-baked bread? How about a nice cut of meat?'"* (Ps. 78:19-20 The Message). So the true reason God fed the Israelites with manna was to test and see their hearts. Sometimes we go through things that God in His infinite wisdom could have stopped, but He allowed them to happen to bring us to a better place in life. Pray the God will give you the true reason behind your life experiences.

Points to Ponder

1. Have you whined about something lately?
2. Do you think it may have been a test of your heart?

GREAT CHALLENGES EQUAL GREAT TESTIMONIES

*You know about them and have heard it said: "Who can stand up against the Anakites?" But be assured today that **the Lord your God is the one who goes across ahead of you like a devouring fire. He will destroy them;** he will subdue them before you. And you will drive them out and annihilate them quickly, as the Lord has promised you"* (Deuteronomy 9:2-3).

I F God is with you, remember, it will turn out for testimony no matter the challenge that may confront you now. God will take the glory out it and He will go ahead of you in every situation like devouring fire consuming every daunting challenge along the way!

Points to Ponder

1. Do you know that God has gone ahead of you to head off the enemy?

2. Have you ever thought of all the troubles that you never knew because God went ahead of you and destroyed them before you even became aware of them?

JESUS—FLESH AND BLOOD

Since the children have flesh and blood, he too shared in their humanity so that by his death he might break the power of him who holds the power of death—that is, the devil—and free those who all their lives were held in slavery by their fear of death. For surely it is not angels he helps, but Abraham's descendants. For this reason he had to be made like them, fully human in every way, in order that he might become a merciful and faithful high priest in service to God, and that he might make atonement for the sins of the people. Because he himself suffered when he was tempted, he is able to help those who are being tempted (Hebrews 2:14-18).

JESUS became human so that through His death He would bring redemption to all people and break the power of the devil. Jesus' sacrifice freed us all from eternal damnation. Jesus was made fully like us in every way—He was tempted, He felt pain, He was hungry, He loved.

Points to Ponder

1. Does knowing that Jesus left His perfect life in Heaven to come to earth and become fully human make a difference in how you perceive Him?

2. In how you praise and worship Him?

The Fullness of God's Blessing

He will love you and bless you and increase your numbers.
He will bless the fruit of your womb, the crops of your land—
your grain, new wine and olive oil—the calves of your herds
and the lambs of your flocks in the land that he swore to your
ancestors to give you. **You will be blessed more than any other**
people; *none of your men or women will be childless, nor any of*
your livestock be without young (Deuteronomy 7:13-14).

THE blessings of God make you rich and add no sorrow. Notice the promises in this passage: blessings all around; wherever you may turn, blessings await you. See the allegory here: *increase in number* refers to expansion and acquisition; *the fruit of your womb* refers to your posterity and the generation after you; *the crops of your land* are the works of your hands and your inheritance; and *the calves of your herd* refers to the management of your wealth.

Points to Ponder

1. Are you living in the fullness of God's blessings?
2. Do you feel blessed more than any others?

THE LORD CREATES WEALTH

But remember the Lord your God, for it is he who gives you the ability to produce wealth... (Deuteronomy 8:18).

WE so often forget the Lord gives ability to whomever He decides. In Him we live, move, and have our being! When you are rich, remember there are many others with similar ideas and potentials but they never had the chance to put their ideas into practice. If you are poor, remember also God can make you rich by opening opportunities—be ever vigilant to recognize these opportunities. By your own strength you will not prevail. Put your confidence in God because every good thing comes from Him.

Points to Ponder

1. Have you become satisfied with your position in life?
2. God is always providing opportunities to move you ahead.
3. Are you watching and eagerly waiting to take advantage of the doors He opens for you?

Reading the Bible in a Year: Judges 10-11 and Luke 9:1-36.

NOT BECAUSE OF YOUR RIGHTEOUSNESS

It is not because of your righteousness or your integrity that you are going in to take possession of their land; but on account of the wickedness of these nations
(Deuteronomy 9:5).

MANY of God's good promises to you are in the possession of other people. God waits for the other people to fill their cups of sin before taking their goods from them. God said the Israelites spent 400 years in slavery because the sins of the Amorites were not yet full. Whenever you are in possession of something good, remember your sins can make you lose it.

Points to Ponder

1. There is much wickedness in many nations worldwide. Do you think the Lord is about ready to take possession of their land?

2. What about your nation?

BEWARE

***Do not bring a detestable thing into your house or you,
like it, will be set apart for destruction.*** *Regard it as vile
and utterly detest it, for it is set apart for destruction*
(Deuteronomy 7:26).

B E mindful of the things and thoughts you allow into your midst.
Things dedicated to idols can be a point of contact for the devil
and his agents to gain access into your household. Evil spirits are ter-
ritorial spirits! They try to claim places in your environment. The
Bible says contamination with accursed things can lead to eventual
destruction. Examine carefully when buying second-hand or used
items; and whenever you get something used, it is a wise move to
pray over it and rededicate it to the Lord.

Points to Ponder

1. Is this a new concept for you to consider?
2. Do you have things previously owned by another that
    may have evil associated with them?
3. Do you need to pray over some things in your home?

_____

_____

_____

Reading the Bible in a Year: Judges 15-17 and Luke 10:1-24.

CHILDREN OF THE LIGHT

For you were once darkness, but now you are light in the Lord.
Live as children of light *(for the fruit of the light consists in*
all goodness, righteousness and truth) (Ephesians 5:8-9).

GOD is the Father of Light. You are light in the midst of gross darkness on earth. Let your Light so shine that the word in you will honor your Father! As light, let goodness, righteousness, and truth radiate from you because these are the fruits of light!

Points to Ponder

1. Do you joyfully accept the role of being a child of the Father of Light?
2. How brightly is your light shining?

IF YOU BELIEVE IT, YOU CAN HAVE IT

And without faith it is impossible to please God, because
anyone who comes to him must believe that he exists and
*that **he rewards those who earnestly seek him***
(Hebrews 11:6).

O FTEN we may not think that we have much to show for the commitment to the things of God, but we are assured of this— our God rewards those who seek Him.

Points to Ponder

1. Are you pleasing God with your faith?
2. Are you earnestly seeking Him? Write ten things that God has rewarded you with lately.

THE REWARDER

He regarded disgrace for the sake of Christ as of greater value than the treasures of Egypt, because he was looking ahead to his reward. By faith he left Egypt, not fearing the king's anger; he persevered because he saw him who is invisible (Hebrews 11:26-27).

I T is better to suffer on the side of righteousness than to run after the joy of momentary pleasure in the wilderness. Today, do not be moved by what you see around you—rather, look up to Him who is invisible, and He will surely reward you.

Points to Ponder

1. Are you looking for your reward everywhere but up?
2. Have you looked up—up beyond the momentary troubles or periodic scuffles of life—to see Him smiling at you?
3. Have you claimed your rewards?

PARTIAL OBEDIENCE IS DISOBEDIENCE

For whoever keeps the whole law and yet stumbles at just one point is guilty of breaking all of it. For he who said, "You shall not commit adultery," also said, "You shall not murder." If you do not commit adultery but do commit murder, you have become a lawbreaker (James 2:10-11).

PARTIAL obedience is disobedience—sober thought! It is easy for us to point at other people's faults or failings, but we forget that we have our own areas of vulnerability. It is referred to as "The sins that so easily besiege us." This is why we must plead the blood of Jesus Christ at all times! For we are strong in some areas—but weak in others.

Points to Ponder

1. Have you read the Ten Commandments lately?
2. Are you guilty of partial obedience? Pray about your weak areas—that God will give you supernatural strength to overcome and obey.

MERCY TRIUMPHS OVER JUDGMENT

Speak and act as those who are going to be judged by the law that gives freedom, because judgment without mercy will be shown to anyone who has not been merciful. Mercy triumphs over judgment (James 2:12-13).

BECAUSE we live in the dispensation of grace, we should not only receive mercy but be prepared to grant others mercy or forgiveness when we have been hurt. The Bible says forgive us our trespasses as we forgive those who trespass against us.

Points to Ponder

1. How merciful are you?
2. Do you quickly or stubbornly offer forgiveness to others?
3. Can you gracefully ask for forgiveness from someone you have wronged?

Spirit of Grace Benefits

Anyone who rejected the law of Moses died without mercy on the testimony of two or three witnesses (Hebrews 10:28).

You have come to God, the Judge of all, to the spirits of righteous made perfect, to Jesus the mediator of a new covenant, and to the sprinkled blood that speaks a better word than the blood of Abel (Hebrews 12:23-24).

IN the dispensation of grace, mercy always triumphs over judgment. In the era of Moses, or the law, people were bound by the laws. But Jesus paid the full price for us! We are free indeed—not to continue in sin and lawlessness, but in the freedom of redeemed righteousness now and forever.

Points to Ponder

1. How easy is it for you to balance freedom and necessary laws?

2. Is it hard for you to reconcile Jesus' statement that He came not to abolish the law but to fulfill it (see Matt. 5:17)?

FAITH, PROMISES, REALITIES

By faith we understand that the universe was formed at God's command, so that what is seen was not made out of what was visible (Hebrews 11:3).

F AITH is the currency with which you are able to transact business in the unseen realm of God. Remember, the things that are seen were made from things not yet visible!

Points to Ponder

1. Do you have faith to see things that are not yet visible?
2. Have you transacted business in the spiritual realm lately?

DON'T LOOK BACK

If they had been thinking of the country they had left, they would have had opportunity to return (Hebrews 11:15).

DON'T look back at the things you have left behind in the world or you will be tempted. The danger of looking back or focusing on the past is the temptation to go backward! The Bible says had they looked back, they may have turned back. On the way to the Promised Land, a land flowing with milk and honey, the Israelites remembered the garlic and the onions they had in Egypt, the land of their slavery. May you overcome the attraction of the past.

Points to Ponder

1. Do you often find yourself thinking of "the good old days"?
2. Were those days really that good?
3. Have you enhanced those days beyond their reality?

LIFE IS DECISION-DRIVEN

*By faith Moses' parents hid him for three months after he was born, because they saw he was no ordinary child, and they were not afraid of the king's edict. By faith Moses, when he had grown up, refused to be known as the son of Pharaoh's daughter. **He chose** to be mistreated along with the people of God rather than to enjoy the fleeting pleasures of sin. He regarded disgrace for the sake of Christ as of greater value than the treasures of Egypt, because **he was looking ahead** to his reward (Hebrews 11:23-26).*

LIFE is sum of the many decisions we make daily! Decisions are the products of thoughts, and the mind is the thought processing venue of our lives. That is why our decisions can transform our lives, because we are transformed by the renewal of our mind! Your thoughts are your seeds for your tomorrows.

Points to Ponder

1. Do you consider carefully every decision you make throughout the day?
2. Do you think about how your next decision may cause God and you great misery or great joy?

KEEP YOUR EYES ON JESUS

*We do this by **keeping our eyes on Jesus,** the champion who initiates and perfects our faith. Because of the joy awaiting him, he endured the cross, disregarding its shame. Now he is seated in the place of honor beside God's throne. **Think of all the hostility he endured from sinful people; then you won't become weary and give up*** (Hebrews 12:2-3 NLT).

JESUS came to this world, that we may have life abundantly. One of the ways we can believe this is to fix our focus on Him and live above the circumstances that may surround us. Consider all He endured and don't give up.

Points to Ponder

1. Do you constantly focus on Jesus?
2. Do you sometimes focus on Jesus?
3. Do you rarely focus on Jesus?

SET YOUR HEARTS AND MINDS

Since, then, you have been raised with Christ, set your hearts on things above, where Christ is, seated at the right hand of God. Set your minds on things above, not on earthly things. For you died, and your life is now hidden with Christ in God (Colossians 3:1-3).

L IFE and issues of life may want to strip virtues out of you. But there is something that can never be taken from you—your ability to make your own decisions! You can decide to set your heart and mind on perishable things and situations around you, or you can choose to set your heart and mind on things eternal. The choice is yours.

Point to Ponder

1. How tempting is it for you to focus on the latest fashion, car, or entertainment attraction rather than set your mind on God and His will for you and your family?

_____

_____

_____

WHAT IS SEEN IS TEMPORARY

So we fix our eyes not on what is seen, but on what is unseen,
since what is seen is temporary, but what is unseen is eternal
(2 Corinthians 4:18).

ACCORDING to this verse in Second Corinthians, we must fix
our eyes not on what is seen, but on what is unseen. For what is
seen is temporary, but what is unseen is eternal.

Points to Ponder

1. What exactly does this verse mean to you personally?
2. What are some temporary things you have been focus-
    ing on lately?
3. What are some eternal things you should be focusing
    on?

THROUGH FAITH

*And what more shall I say? I do not have time to tell about Gideon, Barak, Samson, Jephthah, about David and Samuel and the prophets, who **through faith** conquered kingdoms, administered justice, and gained what was promised; who shut the mouths of lions, quenched the fury of the flames, and escaped the edge of the sword; whose weakness was turned to strength; and who became powerful in battle and routed foreign armies. Women received back their dead, raised to life again. There were others who were tortured, refusing to be released so that they might gain an even better resurrection* (Hebrews 11:32-35).

WE are surrounded by a great cloud of witnesses. Read the Bible and think of the men and women of old and all they accomplished through faith in God. You will be encouraged to fight the fight of life! Let the success of others spin you to achieve greater height in life.

Point to Ponder

1. Are you willing to shut the mouths of lions (stand up to Jesus scoffers), quench the flames (offer a peaceful solution to those red hot tempers), escape the sword (forgive people who cut you with their words or actions), welcome back the dead (greet prodigal sons and daughters), and be tortured (accept criticism, bullying, and violence that some Christians are experiencing worldwide)?

Reading the Bible in a Year: 1 Samuel 25-26 and Luke 16:19-31.

NOT EVERYONE IS BORN OF GOD

You belong to your father, the devil, and you want to carry out your father's desires. He was a murderer from the beginning, not holding to the truth, for there is no truth in him. When he lies, he speaks his native language, for he is a liar and the father of lies (John 8:44).

W E are all created by God, but not all are born of God. The Bible says "there are a people of God." Anytime we disregard God's will and disobey His commands, we are drifting toward the devil. If we do or say things characteristic of the devil we are becoming the sons and daughters of the father of lies.

Points to Ponder

1. Does this verse frighten you?
2. Are you drifting toward the devil or toward God?
3. Are you seeking God's truth and will for your life?

_____

_____

_____

WHEN DARKNESS REIGNS

[Jesus said] *Every day I was with you in the temple courts,
and you did not lay a hand on me. But this is your hour—
when darkness reigns* (Luke 22:53).

I N Ecclesiastes, the Bible says there is time for everything under
the sun. This is one of the most difficult truths to take in, particularly one should accept that darkness can reign sometimes—but
there is always Light at the end of the tunnel.

Points to Ponder

1. Is darkness reigning in your life right now?
2. Maybe there is illness or financial problems in your
   home?
3. Do you believe that God's light will shining brightly
   through any trouble if you only believe?

FROM HERE TO ETERNITY

"Very truly I tell you," Jesus answered, "before Abraham was born, I am!" (John 8:58).

JESUS is eternal. He is the Word who was with God! He is forever with God. He is the One who was slain before the foundations of time. Jesus is the same yesterday, today, and tomorrow.

Point to Ponder

1.   Is there anything anyone could have done to prevent Jesus dying on the cross?

_____

_____

_____

For This Reason I Was Born

"You are a king, then!" said Pilate. Jesus answered, "You say that I am a king. In fact, the reason I was born and came into the world is to testify to the truth. Everyone on the side of truth listens to me" (John 18:37).

THERE is always a reason. Always seek the true reason behind what is happening in your life. Jesus said in the face of death, there is a reason, a divine plan behind the crucifixion! God will take the glory in your life.

Point to Ponder

1. During stressful or hurtful situations, it may be hard to see the reason behind them, but are you willing to search for that reason? No matter how big or small the event, it is worth seeking the reason.

"It Is Finished"

When he had received the drink, Jesus said, "It is finished."
With that, he bowed his head and gave up his spirit
(John 19:30).

I T is finished translates to mean *paid in full!* Your atonement, my atonement was fully completed! If we accept Jesus Christ, all our sins are washed away and we are redeemed, purchased by His blood! All the written laws that convict us were nailed to His cross. He paid our debt in full—"it is finished."

Points to Ponder

1. Is it hard for you to comprehend the level of love Jesus has for you?
2. Can you imagine the suffering He endured to redeem you?
3. What does He expect from you?

A SENSE OF DESTINY

Then Paul answered, "Why are you weeping and breaking my heart? I am ready not only to be bound, but also to die in Jerusalem for the name of the Lord Jesus" (Acts 21:13).

PAUL faced a dilemma! A prophet prophesied in a dramatic tongue that Paul was going to suffer in Jerusalem. The people pleaded with him not to go to Jerusalem, but the Holy Spirit told Paul he should go, despite the suffering he would experience. Paul made the remarkable statement (see verse above) and decided to obey God and go to Jerusalem! Trust and obey—in the end, this is what God expects of all those who love Him.

Points to Ponder

1. Have you ever faced this type of dilemma?
2. What was your decision?
3. Are you willing to trust and obey to the very end?

A SENSE OF DESTINY

However, I consider my life worth nothing to me; my only aim is to finish the race and complete the task the Lord Jesus has given me—the task of testifying to the good news of God's grace (Acts 20:24).

AGAIN, Apostle Paul is saying that he is beyond his own wishes and completely committed to God's will for his life. He wants to fulfill his destiny, which may include facing death.

Points to Ponder

1. How committed are you to finishing the race and complete the task God has given you?
2. Are you running in the race or have you dropped out somewhere along life's journey?

MISPLACED PRIORITY

For they loved human praise more than praise from God
(John 12:43).

THE desire for immediate gratification can blind a person from seeing the full picture. Many a time we all fall victim to this subtle challenge. As the Bible says here in John 12, often we desire the praise of people around us and neglect the fact that ultimately what really counts is the praise of God. The praise of God always comes when doing the will of God. Always seek His praise above all things!

Points to Ponder

1. Are you flattered when someone compliments you?
2. Does it mean more to you than when you do what's right and the only One who knows about it is God?

NOT MY WILL, BUT YOURS

Then he [Jesus] said to them, "My soul is overwhelmed with sorrow to the point of death. Stay here and keep watch with me." Going a little farther, he fell with his face to the ground and prayed, "My Father, if it is possible, may this cup be taken from me. Yet not as I will, but as you will" (Matthew 26:38-39).

JESUS was overwhelmed with sorrow even to the point of death. Yet He still preferred that the will of God be done. This should be our prayer at all times—that God's will be done. No matter the situation we are going through, if we trust and believe, God will turn things out for the best.

Points to Ponder

1. Is it hard to consider that Jesus could be overwhelmed?
2. Does knowing this make the problems you are facing seem easier to handle, or harder?
3. Why or why not?

STREAMS OF LIVING WATER

Whoever believes in me, as the Scripture has said, streams of living water will flow from within them (John 7:38).

ACCORDING to this Scripture in John 7, we can imagine an inexhaustible flow of refreshing and living waters within the redeemed of the Lord—every believer. Yet many born-again Christians walk through life ignorant of this source. Today, remember you have water springing up within you that will keep you from becoming stagnant. Let it flow over yourself and over all those who come near you! Let it flow!

Points to Ponder

1. Are you soaked with the streams of living water flowing from within you?

2. Are you splashing other people around you?

ANOINTING MAKES THE DIFFERENCE

[God said to Moses] *Get Aaron and his son Eleazar and take them up Mount Hor. Remove Aaron's garments and put them on his son Eleazar, for Aaron will be gathered to his people; he will die there* (Numbers 20:25-26).

ANOINTING makes the difference. Aaron could not die until the priestly garment was officially removed from him and given to his son. This is why we must not copy people blindly because they might be protected by the grace of the gift in their lives—the garment of their anointing. Watch carefully, don't be swayed by a crowd mentality.

Points to Ponder

1. Have you ever followed after a crowd and then regretted it?

2. What circumstances caused this lapse in judgment?

SACRIFICE

Gather My saints together to Me, those who have made a covenant with Me by sacrifice (Psalm 50:5 NKJV).

SACRIFICE is forsaking one thing for the greater value of the other. There are sacrifices of obedience, of service, and of the body. Don't neglect any of them. That is why the Bible says God sacrificed His only begotten Son to regain the world (see John 3:16). May you experience uncommon and unprecedented level of favor today!

Points to Ponder

1. Do you routinely make sacrifices for your family?
2. How about at your place of employment?
3. How often do you sacrifice for the sake of God's kingdom?

_____

_____

_____

WILLFUL SIN IS AN ABOMINATION

*If we deliberately keep on sinning after we have received the
knowledge of the truth, no sacrifice for sins is left*
(Hebrews 10:26).

TO know Jesus' sacrifice and ignore Him is to abuse His grace. Sin has a gripping effect and its pleasures can be enticing. God says that premeditated action that the sinner knows is wrong, yet commits anyway for the pleasure of the sin, is willful sin and is an abomination to Him.

Points to Ponder

1. Have you taken deliberate steps to stop sinning now that you know Jesus and His depth of love for you?

2. Or have you been ignoring Him and abusing His grace?

GOD REMEMBERS YOU

*But **God remembered Noah** and all the wild animals and
the livestock that were with him in the ark, and he sent a
wind over the earth, and the waters receded*
(Genesis 8:1, see also 1 Samuel 1:19).

G OD remembers your acts of obedience and adherence to His
principles, which activate your dormant promises—and God
puts the promises into action. When your longstanding promises
are put into motion, it is equivalent to God's remembrance. We are
blessed with all blessings in heavenly places but God actualizes those
promises in our lives when He activates them.

Points to Ponder

1. Are you anticipating some longstanding promises being
    put into motion?
2. Does God have good works and acts of obedience to
    remember about you?

DELIVERED FROM THE MELTING-HOT FURNACE

*But as for you, **the Lord** took you and **brought you out of the iron-smelting furnace**, out of Egypt, to be the people of his inheritance, as you now are* (Deuteronomy 4:20).

A S we are the people of God, be assured that God is able to reach you wherever you are. There is no valley too deep and no mountain too high that He cannot reach out and grab hold of you. The prophet Zechariah saw a vision of God rebuking satan because satan was accusing Joshua. God reminded the devil that Joshua was a stick snatched out of fire, *"The Lord said to Satan, "The Lord rebuke you, Satan! The Lord, who has chosen Jerusalem, rebuke you! Is not this man a burning stick snatched from the fire?"* (Zechariah 3:2).

Points to Ponder

1. Are there too-hot-to-handle situations in your life right now—maybe at work or at church or in a relationship?

2. Who can bring you out of the furnace?

3. How do you know that is possible?

LIFE AND INCREASE
OUT OF DEATH

*And so **from this one man, and he as good as dead, came descendants as numerous as the stars in the sky** and as countless as the sand on the seashore* (Hebrews 11:12).

I N Hebrews 11, the Bible describes Abraham "as good as dead"! Yet out of the loins of this one man came descendants as numerous as the stars of the sky. May God bring fruitfulness out of every dead situation around you!

Points to Ponder

1. Do you sometimes feel "as good as dead"?
2. What must you do to become fruitful and alive again?

GOD'S POWERFUL WORD BRINGS INCREASE

So the word of God spread. The number of disciples in Jerusalem increased rapidly, and a large number of priests became obedient to the faith (Acts 6:7).

THE word is sharper than a two-edged sword, *"For the word of God is living and powerful, and sharper than any two-edged sword, piercing even to the division of soul and spirit, and of joints and marrow, and is a discerner of the thoughts and intents of the heart"* (Heb. 4:12). As the word spread, the number of disciples increased. Anything you speak the word to increases. Anything you speak the word to aligns with destiny and the purpose of God!

Points to Ponder

1. How comfortable are you spreading God's word?
2. Have people rebuked you for sharing the Good News with them?
3. Did their rebuke strengthen or weaken you?

_____

_____

_____

FATHERHOOD AND FATHERING

"Tell me about your father, young man," Saul said. And David replied, "His name is Jesse, and we live in Bethlehem" (1 Samuel 17:58 NLT).

SAUL asked David a curious question after he killed Goliath the giant, after he had done what no one else could do and brought a great victory to Israel. In the Scripture verse, Saul seems to imply that David's victory over Goliath is connected with who his father is. Fatherhood and fathering is a divine order of love and covering. You are special to God your Father in Heaven—Father of us all. It is my prayer that the Lord will richly bless all parents today and every day.

Points to Ponder

1. Many people had less-than-ideal parents growing up—how about you?
2. If you had loving parents, have you thanked them lately?
3. Have you thanked God for His fatherly place in your life lately?

THE FATHER OF YOUR SPIRIT

Moreover, we have all had human fathers who disciplined us and we respected them for it. How much more should we submit to the Father of spirits and live! (Hebrews 12:9)

THOUGH our spirits may be invisible, yet they are the essence and center of humankind. Our spirits bear witness with the Spirit of God. Whenever we submit to the Spirit of God, we gain life.

Points to Ponder

1. Did you rebel against the discipline of your natural father?

2. Do you rebel against your heavenly Father?

3. Why or why not?

Easy for God

*Dig ditches all over this valley. Here's what will happen, you won't hear the wind, you won't see the rain, but this valley is going to fill up with water and your army and your animals will drink their fill. **This is easy for God to do**; he will also hand over Moab to you. You will ravage the country: Knock out its fortifications...* (2 Kings 3:16 The Message).

SOMETIMES, we are so focused on the ways of the world, its systems, and its methodology that we lose sight of the superior system of God. There was a drought, no water for the animals. People wanted to see the cloud gather and the wind blow and then the rain fall. That is the normal expectation. But rather the prophet said "dig ditches" to collect water because even though there will be no the cloud, winds, or rain, the ditches shall be full of water! God will omit some unnecessary stages to bring you your destiny. Today go, prepare, and receive your miracle; this is a small thing in the eyes of God!

Points to Ponder

1. If God told you to do something that seemed odd or unrealistic, would you obey Him?
2. Would you question Him?
3. Would you doubt Him?

THE BLESSING OF GOSHEN

Now the Israelites settled in Egypt in the region of Goshen.
They acquired property there and were fruitful and increased
greatly in number (Genesis 47:27).

GOSHEN is a special place and a place of blessing for the people of God. It was a place chosen, nurtured, and protected by God. In the days the Jews were in Egypt, they saw the blessings of Goshen. When Egypt was in darkness, Goshen had light, when Egypt suffered economic woes, Goshen experienced economic prosperity. We are in the season of Goshen blessings!

May the blessings of heaven and earth rest upon you! May you acquire property, be fruitful and increase greatly—you and your family. *"**May the Lord bless your land** with the precious dew from Heaven above and with the deep waters that lie below; with the best the sun brings forth and the finest the moon can yield; with the choicest gifts of the ancient mountains and the fruitfulness of the everlasting hills; with the best gifts of the earth and its fullness and the favor of Him who dwelt in the burning bush..."* (Deut. 33:13-16).

Points to Ponder

1. Are you tired of the darkness of economic woes?
2. Are you ready to live in a place of fruitfulness and increase?

THE LORD WILL DELIVER YOU

You will not have to fight this battle. Take up your position;
stand firm and see the deliverance the Lord will give you!
(2 Samuel 20:17)

THIS is what Jehoshaphat said to the Israelites when a vast army came against them. This also is my decree to you today! You will not have to lift a finger—just *stand firm.* Spiritual warfare is sweet if we play by God's rules. It actually means we take our stand in God and watch Him fight our battles. That is why He said, *"Be still, and know that I am God"* (Ps. 46:10). He is a man of war—and great victories!

Points to Ponder

1. Are you patient enough to stand firm?
2. Can you be still enough to see the Lord fight your battles?
3. Are you too eager to fight your own battles?

VENGEANCE BELONGS TO GOD

*For we know him who said, "It is mine to avenge; I will repay," and again, "**The Lord will judge his people**"* (Hebrews 10:30).

*For **the Lord will vindicate his people** and have compassion on his servants* (Psalm 135:14).

V ENGEANCE belongs to God! It is hard to resist the temptation of taking the law into our hands and repaying people for the wrong done to us.

Points to Ponder

1.   Have you ever sought revenge yourself?
2.   Have you felt regret or remorse after taking revenge on someone who wronged you?

SET FREE BY THE TRUTH

*Then you will know the truth, and **the truth will set you free***
(John 8:32).

THE truth has power! No limitation can hold back the power of the truth. Today if you are at a loss which way to go, always choose the path of the truth no matter how it seems, it is guaranteed to see you through.

Points to Ponder

1. When the truth, or the right thing to do, is too hard, do you sometimes take the easy way out?

2. Do you always try and do what the Holy Spirit is nudging you to do?

The Armor of His Light

The night is nearly over; the day is almost here. So let us put aside the deeds of darkness and put on the armour of light. Let us behave decently, as in the daytime, not in orgies and drunkenness, not in sexual immorality and debauchery, not in dissension and jealousy. Rather, clothe yourselves with the Lord Jesus Christ, and do not think about how to gratify the desires of the flesh (Romans 13:12-14).

LIGHT is armor! Whenever you choose light rather than darkness, you come into God's protection. Put *off* the deeds of darkness such drunkenness, sexual immorality, jealousy and bitterness. Put *on* the armor of light. Today choose Light!

Points to Ponder

1. Have you been haunted with addictions that lead to sin?
2. Have you been serious about putting off deeds of darkness and putting on the armor of His Light?

No

There is no divination against Jacob,
no evil omens against Israel (Numbers 23:23).

NO sorcery, no witchcraft, no spell, no incantation, and no divination can work against you! Why? Because the Lord is with you always. Do not cause any crack in your armor by allowing these sources of the devil to tempt you.

Points to Ponder

1. Do you check your horoscope every day?
2. Do you think this is where you will find God's will for your life?
3. What is a better way to search for your God-given destiny?

_____

_____

_____

LET THE LIGHT SHINE

*You, Lord, keep my lamp burning; my **God turns my darkness into light*** (Psalm 18:28).

GOD brings us out "into a spacious place" (Ps. 18:19) full of His bright glory. Light dawns for us even in darkness: this is our portion!

Points to Ponder

1. Do you sometimes feel as if the walls of your soul are closing in and taking you to a dark place?
2. Who can you turn to when that happens?
3. Is God capable of keeping your spirit's lamp burning brightly?

PLEASANT PLACES

Lord, you alone are my portion and my cup; you make my lot secure. The boundary lines have fallen for me in pleasant places; surely I have a delightful inheritance (Psalm 16:5-6).

THE choice portion is your allotment because the Maker of Heaven and earth has decided to handpick your destiny of abundant favor. Concentrating on such wonderful blessings will lift your spirit and give you hope. Who doesn't want to walk into a delightful inheritance?

Points to Ponder

1. Is there a special place where you feel safe and secure?
2. Is it in your home? Church? A nearby park?
3. God will meet you wherever you are—do you believe that?

ALLOW THE LORD TO DIRECT YOU

Whether you turn to the right or to the left, your ears will hear a voice behind you, saying, "This is the way; walk in it" (Isaiah 30:21).

Direct my footsteps according to your word; let no sin rule over me (Psalm 119:133).

THE Lord will direct your ways and your steps will be ordered by the Lord! His direction in your life counts above all things; remember, He knows the end from the beginning.

Points to Ponder

1. Are you hurrying along in life so quickly that you don't hear His voice behind you telling you the way?

2. Are your footsteps going toward God's word or toward sin?

FOOLISHNESS AND VINDICTIVENESS

Now David had been told, "Ahithophel is among the conspirators with Absalom." So David prayed, "Lord, turn Ahithophel's counsel into foolishness" (2 Samuel 15:31).

EVERY counsel of Ahithophel (whether we know it or not) shall be turned into foolishness. The spirit of Ahithophel (conspirators against God) is always associated with those who have a spirit of vindictiveness. Both foolishness and vindictiveness must be defeated in your life.

Points to Ponder

1. Have you been described as being vindictive or foolish?
2. Instead, do people come to you for godly counsel because you are wise and forgiving?

HE KNOWS ALL PEOPLE

But Jesus would not entrust himself to them,
for he knew all people (John 2:24).

GOD doesn't need someone's unjust testimony about another person. Whatever malicious people may say about you, you can rest assured of this—God does not need their testimony about you. *His* opinion of you is what counts.

Points to Ponder

1. Are you reassured that God knows the truth about you?
2. Are you thankful that He knows your heart and your motivations?

COMPLETE FAITH

*You see that his faith and his actions were working together,
and his **faith was made complete** by what he did*
(James 2:22).

FAITH without work (action) is dead. If you have faith today in something, prove it by the work you do with it.

Points to Ponder

1. Do you agree that faith without works is dead faith?
2. What work or action comes to mind when you think about living faith?

THE LORD GAVE THEM UP

How could one man chase a thousand, or two put ten thousand to flight, unless their Rock had sold them, unless the Lord had given them up? (Deuteronomy 32:30)

THE fact of the matter is that this verse in Deuteronomy is more than mere mathematical summation, it entails two-phased grace: on one hand, it is the strengthening of *two* as they rout the *ten thousand*, but more than that it involves the *grace of God* that weakened the ten thousand; He sold them out to be defeated. The Lord can set your enemies running too!

Points to Ponder

1. Would you like to see your foes fleeing from your sight?
2. Do you believe the Lord can put every person to flight who is working against your God-given destiny?

As Many as the Stars in the Sky

The Lord your God has increased your numbers so that today you are as numerous as the stars in the sky. May the Lord, the God of your ancestors, increase you a thousand times and bless you as he has promised! (Deuteronomy 1:10-11)

THIS is the anointing for a *thousand-fold increase!* May God increase you a thousand-fold and bless you as He has promised. When God increases, it is not only in one area but in all aspects of your life—spiritually, emotionally, materially, and in holiness and righteousness. Think of all you can achieve with a thousand times more righteousness or thinking God's thoughts and acting more Christ-likeness a thousand times more.

Points to Ponder

1. If you had a thousand times more love for others, how would your life change?
2. How would your family's lives change?
3. How would your workplace change?

LOVE FULFILLS THE LAW OF LIFE

*The commandments, "You shall not commit adultery," "You shall not murder," "You shall not steal," "You shall not covet," and whatever other command there may be, are summed up in this one command: "Love your neighbor as yourself." Love does no harm to a neighbor. Therefore **love is the fulfillment of the law** (Romans 13:9-10).*

T HE Bible is full of love verses because love is the key to all of life—relationships, emotional and mental stability, good health, and the basis of Christianity. Consider these additional verses from Romans: *"Let no debt remain outstanding, except the continuing debt to **love one another**, for whoever loves others has fulfilled the law"* (Rom. 13:8). *"For none of us lives for ourselves alone, and none of us dies for ourselves alone"* (Rom. 14:7).

Points to Ponder

1. Are you as lovable as you could be?
2. Do you try and show love to all those with whom you come in contact?
3. What can you do to become more lovable?

WITH ALL YOUR HEART AND SOUL

*But be very careful to keep the commandment and the law
that Moses the servant of the Lord gave you: to love the Lord
your God, to walk in obedience to him, to obey his commands,
to hold fast to him and to serve him with all your heart and
all your soul* (Joshua 22:5).

G OD requires that you love Him, obey Him, and serve Him.
Considering all that He has done for us, these commands are
wholly justified. When others look at us, they should see people
totally committed to Him in body, mind, and spirit.

Point to Ponder

1. Are you committed to loving Him, obeying Him, and
    serving Him with all your heart and all your soul?

HIS BLESSINGS

...he blessed them, saying, "Return to your homes with your great wealth—with large herds of livestock, with silver, gold, bronze and iron, and a great quantity of clothing—and divide the plunder from your enemies with your fellow Israelites"
(Joshua 22:7-8).

THE Lord was with His people and caused them to gain great wealth. He is also with us and desires us to have great wealth at the expense of our enemies. In His timing and His justice, we will attain all that He has for us.

Points to Ponder

1. What is your idea of "great wealth"?
2. What is your idea of His blessings?
3. Do your ideas include good health, peaceful family relationships, a contented heart?

A SENSE OF PURPOSE

He has made everything beautiful in its time. He also has planted eternity in men's hearts and minds [a divinely implanted sense of a purpose working through the ages which nothing under the sun but God alone can satisfy], yet so that men cannot find out what God has done from the beginning to the end (Ecclesiastes 3:11 AMP).

GOD has planted a sense of purpose in you that is uniquely yours to fulfill. You are unlike anyone else on the earth. Your purpose works in direct harmony with God's divine plan for your generation—a plan to expand His Kingdom on earth as it is in Heaven.

Points to Ponder

1. Are you an active participant in God's plan by fulfilling your special purpose?

2. Why or why not?

DESTINY'S PROCESS

*So he passed through the hill country of Ephraim and through the area around Shalisha, but they did not find them. They went on into the district of Shaalim, **but the donkeys were not there**. Then he passed through the territory of Benjamin, **but they did not find them**. When they reached the district of Zuph, Saul said to the servant who was with him, "Come, let's go back, or my father will stop thinking about the donkeys and start worrying about us." But the servant replied, "Look, in this town there is **a man of God; he is highly respected, and everything he says comes true**. Let's go there now. Perhaps he will tell us what way to take" (1 Samuel 9:4-6).*

THIS mission to find the donkeys was ultimately not about the donkeys at all, the search was just part of the process of bringing Saul to his destiny. God uses various circumstances, people, and opportunities to bring us to our destiny. We are all on a life journey as part of the process of bringing our God-given destiny to fruition.

Points to Ponder

1. Are you on a seemingly futile search for donkeys?
2. Have you considered that your mission is ultimately leading you to some place or someone who is part of destiny's process?

THE VOICE OF GOD

*A third time **the Lord called,** "Samuel!" And Samuel got up and went to Eli and said, "Here I am; you called me." Then Eli realized that **the Lord was calling** the boy. So Eli told Samuel, "Go and lie down, and if he calls you, say, 'Speak, Lord, for your servant is listening.'" So Samuel went and lay down in his place. **The Lord came** and stood there, calling as at the other times, "Samuel! Samuel!" Then Samuel said, "Speak, for your servant is listening"* (1 Samuel 3:8-10).

SOMETIMES the Lord will call us and we don't recognize His voice. Sometimes the Lord calls us through others and we don't recognize Him. Sometimes the Lord wants us to lay down and listen. As Samuel did, let us take time to lay down, quiet ourselves, and say to Him, "Speak, for your servant is listening."

Points to Ponder

1. When is the last time you devoted quiet time for listening to the Lord?
2. Have you taken time to hear His voice lately?
3. What is more important than waiting for the Lord to speak to you?

THE ESSENCE OF A PROPHET

The Lord was with Samuel as he grew up, and he let none of Samuel's words fall to the ground. And all Israel from Dan to Beersheba recognized that Samuel was attested as a prophet of the Lord (1 Samuel 3:19-20).

B ECAUSE Samuel quieted himself and listened for the voice of God, the Lord "was with Samuel as he grew up." No matter how old we are, God will be with us as we grow up, as we mature in the faith.

Points to Ponder

1. Are you maturing in your faith in God?
2. Are there positive signs that you have grown up from when you first came to know Jesus as your personal Lord and Savior?

"THE LORD HELPED US"

*Then Samuel took a stone and set it up between Mizpah and Shen. He named it Ebenezer, saying, "Thus far has **the Lord helped us.**" So the Philistines were subdued and they stopped invading Israel's territory. Throughout Samuel's lifetime, the hand of the Lord was against the Philistines* (1 Samuel 7:12-13).

SAMUEL became a voice for the Lord to His people. He placed a marker showing how the Lord had helped in time of need. He called it Ebenezer. The Lord will help us too. He will raise His hand against our enemies and stop them from invading our territory.

Point to Ponder

1. Do you have "markers" tucked into your Bible or scribbled in a journal showing how the Lord has helped you in times of need? If not, think about starting a collection of remembrances of God's blessings.

GOD LOOKS AT THE HEART

But the Lord said to Samuel, "Do not consider his appearance or his height, for I have rejected him. The Lord does not look at the things people look at. People look at the outward appearance, but the LORD looks at the heart" (1 Samuel 16:7).

LOOKS can be deceptive and things may not be what they seem—to us. But whatever God looks at, He discerns reality. We must try to see people and situations through God's eyes, through love's eyes.

Points to Ponder

1. Have you mistakenly judged someone by the way he or she looks?

2. Has anyone ever misjudged you by the way you look?

3. How did that make you feel?

WHAT'S AGE GOT TO DO WITH IT?

*Jesse had seven of his sons pass before Samuel, but Samuel said to him, "The Lord has not chosen these." So he asked Jesse, "Are these all the sons you have?" "There is still the youngest," Jesse answered. "He is tending the sheep." Samuel said, "Send for him; we will not sit down until he arrives." So he sent for him and had him brought in. He was glowing with health and had a fine appearance and handsome features. Then the Lord said, "Rise and anoint him; **this is the one**" (1 Samuel 16:10-12).*

I N the natural, this "youngest" could not possibly be the one! His father did not think he would be the one, and no doubt his brothers did not think so either. But the ceremony was suspended until David arrived from the field and God anointed him king! God can use anyone, anytime, at any age.

Points to Ponder

1. Have you been a victim of age discrimination in the workplace, the church, at home?

2. Have you judged someone because of their age?

THE ANOINTING, THE SPIRIT, AND THE POWER

So Samuel took the horn of oil and anointed him in the presence of his brothers, and from that day on the Spirit of the Lord came powerfully upon David (1 Samuel 16:13).

WHENEVER the Spirit comes, power and anointing are displayed! The anointing is the power and outward expression of the presence of the Holy Spirit. David went on to do great things for the Lord—and for us as he wrote most of the Psalms, which have brought comfort and encouragement for millions of people worldwide for generations upon generations.

Point to Ponder

1. The same Spirit of the Lord is available to you today—are you seeking the anointing and the power from Him?

CHOSEN PEOPLE

*But you are a **chosen people**, a royal priesthood, a holy nation, God's special possession, that you may declare the praises of him who called you out of darkness into his wonderful light* (1 Peter 2:9).

B ELIEVERS the world round are His chosen people—we belong to Him and are citizens of His holy nation. As the Leader of His blessed nation, He rules with righteousness and justice for all. His commandments should be proclaimed as the perfect foundation for every nation of the world.

Points to Ponder

1. Have you declared the praises of God who called you out of darkness into His wonderful light?

2. Have you declared your allegiance to this great nation of His?

_____

_____

_____

TEMPTATION AND EVIL THOUGHTS

And remember when someone wants to do wrong it is never God who is tempting him, for God never wants to do wrong and never tempts anyone else to do it. Temptation is the pull of man's own evil thoughts and wishes. These evil thoughts lead to evil action and afterward to the death penalty from God (James 1:13-15 Living Bible).

W HEN you are tempted to do wrong, you must quickly shove evil thoughts from your mind and spirit. Do not allow even a moment of temptation to turn into thoughts that will corrupt your body, mind, and spirit. Immediately turn to God and ask Him for His power to overcome the temptation.

Points to Ponder

1. How hard is it for you to avoid temptation?
2. If there are certain places or people who tempt you, do you ask God for the courage to stay away from them?

DON'T LIVE IN THE PAST

The Lord said to Samuel, "How long will you mourn for Saul, since I have rejected him as king over Israel? Fill your horn with oil and be on your way; I am sending you to Jesse of Bethlehem. I have chosen one of his sons to be king" (1 Samuel 16:1).

T HE Lord has a new greater and better assignment for you. Don't get caught up with what should have been. Fill your horn with oil, get up; your anointing still stands and there are lives to be turned.

Points to Ponder

1. Are you guilty of living in the past?
2. Do past events, pains, or loves hinder you from moving forward?

FIVE-DAY PRAYER AND FASTING
DAY ONE

F OR the next five days, I encourage you to fast—sacrifice—something you enjoy to show your devotion to God. Today's Scripture focus to pray on is: *"Have mercy on me, O God, according to your unfailing love; according to your great compassion blot out my transgressions. Wash away all my iniquity and cleanse me from my sin. Create in me a pure heart, O God, and renew a steadfast spirit within me"* (Psalm 51:1-2,10).

Points to Ponder

1.   What are you going to fast from?
2.   Why is this fast special to you?
3.   What does this Scripture passage mean to you?

_____

_____

_____

FIVE-DAY PRAYER AND FASTING
DAY TWO

F OR the next four days, I encourage you to fast—sacrifice—something you enjoy to show your devotion to God. Today's Scripture focus to pray on is: *"You will not have to fight this battle. Take up your positions; stand firm and see the deliverance the Lord will give you, Judah and Jerusalem. Do not be afraid; do not be discouraged. Go out to face them tomorrow, and the Lord will be with you"* (2 Chronicles 20:17).

Points to Ponder

1. What are you going to fast from today?
2. Why is this fast special to you?
3. What does this Scripture passage mean to you?

_____

_____

_____

FIVE-DAY PRAYER AND FASTING
DAY THREE

F OR the next three days, I encourage you to fast—sacrifice—something you enjoy to show your devotion to God. Today's Scripture focus to pray on is: *"He thwarts the plans of the crafty, so that their hands achieve no success. He catches the wise in their craftiness, and the schemes of the wily are swept away"* (Job 5:12-13).

Points to Ponder

1. What are you going to fast from today?
2. Why is this fast special to you?
3. What does this Scripture passage mean to you?

_____

_____

_____

FIVE-DAY PRAYER AND FASTING
DAY FOUR

FOR the next two days, I encourage you to fast—sacrifice—something you enjoy to show your devotion to God. Today's Scripture focus to pray on is: *"There is no wisdom, no insight, no plan that can succeed against the Lord"* [and His plans for you!] (Proverbs 21:30).

Points to Ponder

1. What are you going to fast from today?
2. Why is this fast special to you?
3. What does this Scripture passage mean to you?

Reading the Bible in a Year: 2 Chronicles 29-31 and John 18:1-23.

FIVE-DAY PRAYER AND FASTING
DAY FIVE

FOR today, I encourage you to fast—sacrifice—something you enjoy to show your devotion to God. Today's Scripture focus to pray on is: *"May the favor of the Lord our God rest on us; establish the work of our hands for us—yes, establish the work of our hands"* (Psalm 90:17).

Points to Ponder

1.   What are you going to fast from today?
2.   Why is this fast special to you?
3.   What does this Scripture passage mean to you?

THE SACRIFICE OF PRAISE

*Through him then let us continually offer up a **sacrifice of praise** to God, that is, the fruit of lips that acknowledge his name* (Hebrews 13:15 Living Bible).

GOD is worthy of our praise, our sacrifice. When considering what God did for us through the death and resurrection of Christ Jesus, our sacrifice of praise and worship is an honor and a privilege for us. So worthy is He!

Points to Ponder

1. Do you routinely praise God with all your heart?
2. Is praise and worship to God Almighty a regular part of your day?
3. How sweet is the fruit of your lips in praise to Him?

_____

_____

_____

ALL THAT IS GOOD AND PERFECT

*Every good and perfect gift is from above, coming down
from the Father of the heavenly lights, who does not change
like shifting shadows* (James 1:17).

GOD is the giver of every good and perfect gift. He is the ultimate gift-giver. He never has to worry about giving the wrong size or the wrong color. He isn't concerned about the birth date or the holiday season. His gifts come down continually to shower His children with exactly what they need at the perfect time.

Points to Ponder

1. Is your gift-giving a time of frustration or are you filled with joy?
2. Do you struggle with finding the "perfect gift" for someone(s)?
3. How often do you thank God for "every good and perfect gift" from above?

_____

_____

_____

PRODUCING PERSEVERANCE

Consider it pure joy, my brothers and sisters, whenever you face trials of many kinds, because you know that the testing of your faith produces perseverance. Let perseverance finish its work so that you may be mature and complete, not lacking anything (James 1:2-4).

N O one likes to face trials of *any* kind, and especially of *"many kinds."* But unlike unbelievers, believers can face our trials confidently because we know that the testing of our faith produces perseverance, which leads to a life of God's abundance. Perseverance is another word for diligence, determination, and persistence—all qualities that bring success into every corner of your life.

Points to Ponder

1. Are you a determined person?
2. Do you allow trials to get you down or lift you up?

MAY THE HEAVENS AND EARTH BLESS YOU

*...**May the Lord bless** his land with the precious dew from heaven above and with the deep waters that lie below; with the best the sun brings forth and the finest the moon can yield; with the choicest gifts of the ancient mountains and the fruitfulness of the everlasting hills; with the best gifts of the earth and its fullness and the favor of him who dwelt in the burning bush...* (Deuteronomy 33:13-16).

THE Lord is ready to bless you in so very many ways. He loves you so much that he uses His creation to bless you—from the rain and the oceans and rivers to the sun and the moon. He uses the towering mountains and the fruit trees and the meadows to show His greatness to all who come to Him with an open heart and a trusting spirit.

Points to Ponder

1. How has God used nature to bring you closer to Him?
2. Are you awed by the expanse of His love for you?

_____

_____

_____

Reading the Bible in a Year: Ezra 6-8 and John 21.

CHOOSE LIFE

*This day I call the heavens and the earth as witnesses against you that I have set before you life and death, blessings and curses. Now **choose life,** so that you and your **children may live*** (Deuteronomy 30:19).

L IFE is precious to God. All life is born of Him—He creates all living humans, creatures, plants, and animals. Life begins with God. In this world is life and death, blessings and curses. We can choose life and blessings; and when we do, our children will live.

Points to Ponder

1. Do you agree that we live in an age of death?
2. Societies are quick to glorify the "right to chose," but is that choice for life or death?
3. So that children may live, or die? Your thoughts?

YOU ARE ACCOUNTABLE

*The Lord our God has secrets known to no one. We are not accountable for them, but **we and our children are accountable forever for all that he has revealed to us**, so that we may obey all the terms of these instructions* (Deuteronomy 29:29 NLT).

WE will be held accountable by God for what has revealed to us. While on this earth, mysteries will remain, but God has revealed His will to us in various ways and at various times throughout our lives. His revelations are to be taken seriously and considered thoughtfully—so we can obey His commands, which are for our benefit.

Points to Ponder

1. What are some of the things God has revealed to you, such as what you know in your heart is right and wrong?

2. What issues prick your heart when you think of them?

_____

_____

_____

BLESSING OR CURSE

See, I am setting before you today a blessing and a curse—the blessing if you obey the commands of the Lord your God that I am giving you today; the curse if you disobey the commands of the Lord your God and turn from the way that I command you today by following other gods, which you have not known (Deuteronomy 11:26-28).

THE choice is ours. We will receive the blessing if we obey God's commands. We will receive a curse if we disobey His commands. We are told not to follow after other gods, which include anything that take priority away from God's will for our lives. We much chose God's blessing on our lives to enjoy all that He has for us.

Points to Ponder

1. Are you happy with the choices you have made in life?
2. If not, what can you do to ensure making good choices in the future?

PLACE GOD'S WORD IN YOUR HEART

Fix these words of mine in your hearts and minds; tie them as symbols on your hands and bind them on your foreheads. Teach them to your children, talking about them when you sit at home and when you walk along the road, when you lie down and when you get up. Write them on the doorframes of your houses and on your gates, so that your days and the days of your children may be many in the land that the Lord swore to give your forefathers, as many as the days that the heavens are above the earth (Deuteronomy 11:18-21).

GOD is commanding us to absorb His word into every part of our lives and into the lives of our children, our homes, and our neighbourhoods. Our days and the days of our children will be long if we obey Him. He knows that if we obey His word, our lives will be victorious and full of peace and joy. Only He can bring such even in the midst of life's inevitable trials.

Points to Ponder

1. Do you routinely talk about God with your children?
2. Do you routinely talk about God when you are at work?
3. Do you routinely think about and pray to God before you go to bed and before you get out of bed each morning?

YOU WILL BE SATISFIED

So if you faithfully obey the commands I am giving you
today—to love the Lord your God and to serve him with all
your heart and with all your soul—then I will send rain on
your land in its season, both autumn and spring rains, so
that you may gather in your grain, new wine and oil. I will
*provide grass in the fields for your cattle, and **you will eat***
and be satisfied (Deuteronomy 11:13-15).

HOW clear it is in this passage from Deuteronomy 11 that if
we faithfully obey God's commands He will send us life-giving
nourishment. All we have to do is love Him with all our hearts and
souls. How easy it should be for us to love Him because of all He has
done for us, all He has sacrificed for us, all He desires to give us still.

Points to Ponder

1. Have you eaten of the world and remain hungry?
2. Have you eaten of what others give you and remain
   hungry?
3. Do you know now that only God completely satisfies
   every hunger?

_____

_____

_____

NOURISHMENT FROM GOD

*When she heard in Moab that the Lord had come to the aid of
his people by providing food for them, Naomi and her daughters-
in-law prepared to return home from there* (Ruth 1:6).

NEWS traveled fast that God was providing food for hungry
people. Naomi and her two daughters-in-law decided to go
home—back to where their hunger would be satisfied. During the
trip, one daughter-in-law decided not to proceed, but Ruth stayed
with her mother-in-law. Doing so brought her not only food for her
physical body but spiritual food that led her into the house of Boaz
and the lineage of the house of David.

Points to Ponder

1. When you eat from God's table, do you expect more
    than just physical food?

2. When you accept sustenance from the Lord, do you
    expect more than a quick fill-up?

"Don't be Afraid"

But Joseph said to them, "Don't be afraid. Am I in the place of God? You intended to harm me, but God intended it for good to accomplish what is now being done, the saving of many lives. So then, don't be afraid. I will provide for you and your children." And he reassured them and spoke kindly to them (Genesis 50:19-21).

JOSEPH said first, "Don't be afraid." He put his brothers' minds at ease that he held no grudge, he knew God was using their unkind and unjust act of selling him into slavery to accomplish God's plan to save many lives. Joseph even spoke kindly to them. Joseph is a model of forgiveness and love. We should study Joseph's life and use it as an example of who we can be if we focus on God—as did Joseph through all his trials and troubles.

Points to Ponder

1. Are there people you need to forgive and to whom you need to speak kindly?

2. Is your heart big enough to see God's plan in even the worst of circumstances?

WHO IS COVERING YOU?

The men said to her, "This oath you made us swear will not be binding on us unless, when we enter the land, you have tied this scarlet cord in the window through which you let us down, and unless you have brought your father and mother, your brothers and all your family into your house. If any of them go outside your house into the street, their blood will be on their own heads; we will not be responsible. As for those who are in the house with you, their blood will be on our head if a hand is laid on him. But if you tell what we are doing, we will be released from the oath you made us swear" (Joshua 2:17-20).

T HE two spies Joshua sent made an oath with Rahab. She and her family would be safe if they obeyed the instructions. The spies took responsibility for the family's safety and protection—if they complied with the oath made between them with Rahab. Any member of her family who remained in the house would be covered and protected. The story has a happy ending for Rahab and her family—they knew whose side they were on.

Points to Ponder

1. Who is covering, protecting you?
2. Do you rely on external forces that may or may not show up in time?
3. Do you rely on the Internal and Eternal Force who is always front and center forging a safe path for you to tread?

_____

_____

MELTING IN FEAR

Then the two men started back. They went down out of the hills, forded the river and came to Joshua son of Nun and told him everything that had happened to them. They said to Joshua, "The Lord as surely given the whole land into our hands; all the people are melting in fear because of us" (Joshua 2:23-24).

THE spies who made an oath with Rahab returned to Joshua with a good report. The enemies were "melting in fear." Truly when God is for us, no one can stand against us. Believing in the Lord is makes us strong—fear makes people melt away.

Point to Ponder

1. Are you standing strong for Jesus, for all things right-eous—or melting away in fear of what someone might think or say about you?

YOU HAVE NEVER BEEN THIS WAY BEFORE

*giving orders to the people: "When you see the ark of the covenant of the Lord your God, and the Levitical priests carrying it, you are to **move out from your positions and follow** it. Then you will know which way to go, since **you have never been this way before.** But keep a distance of about two thousand cubits between you and the ark; do not go near it"* (Joshua 3:3-4).

SOMETIMES God has us travel to places and experience events that are new to us. Sometimes He has us move from our positions and follow a new path. We must be willing to trust Him and His direction for our lives—no matter if we have never been that way before.

Points to Ponder

1. Does moving in a different direction make you fearful?
2. Are you excited about changes and new experiences?
3. How can you prepare yourself for whatever God may have in store for you?

DIVINE BREAKTHROUGH

*Joshua told the people, "**Consecrate yourselves,** for tomorrow the Lord will do amazing things among you"* (Joshua 3:5).

CONSECRATION is a prerequisite for divine breakthrough. Consecration means to humble and dedicate ourselves before the Lord. Pride and self-gratification have no place in our hearts and minds if we are to see God do amazing things in our lives and in the lives of our loved ones.

Points to Ponder

1. How do you consecrate yourself before the Lord?
2. Are you eager for a divine breakthrough?

THE LORD OF ALL THE EARTH

*This is how you will know that the living God is among you and that **he will certainly drive out before you** the Canaanites, Hittites, Hivites, Perizzites, Girgashites, Amorites and Jebusites. See, the ark of the covenant of the Lord of all the earth will go into the Jordan ahead of you. Now then, choose twelve men from the tribes of Israel, one from each tribe. And as soon as the priests who carry the ark of the Lord—**the Lord of all the earth**—set foot in the Jordan, its waters flowing downstream will be cut off and stand up in a heap* (Joshua 3:10-13).

OUR victories should testify of God's mercy and grace. Because He is the One who drives out our enemies before us, we must learn to praise and worship Him as the Lord of all the earth. Enemies can come in all shapes and sizes—physical, spiritual, emotional, relational—and only God has the power and wisdom to defeat each and every one for you.

Points to Ponder

1. What enemy are you facing today?
2. Do you believe that God, for His glory, has already defeated that enemy?

PROMOTION COMES FROM GOD

*And the Lord said to Joshua, "Today **I will begin to exalt you**
in the eyes of all Israel, so they may know that I am with you
as I was with Moses." That day **the Lord exalted Joshua** in the
sight of all Israel; and they stood in awe of him all the days of his
life, just as they had stood in awe of Moses (Joshua 3:7; 4:14).*

T HE Lord promoted Joshua and everyone noticed it. Joshua was
favored by God because he had been obedient in all that the
Lord required of him. Joshua became a great leader, following in the
footsteps of Moses.

Points to Ponder

1. Are you deserving of promotion in God's army?
2. Are you patiently waiting for a promotion in the workplace? At church?
3. When the time is right, do you believe that the Lord will
   advance you into the proper position?

_____

_____

_____

IN REVERENCE

Now when Joshua was near Jericho, he looked up and saw a man standing in front of him with a drawn sword in his hand. Joshua went up to him and asked, "Are you for us or for our enemies?" "Neither," he replied, "but as commander of the army of the Lord, I have now come." Then Joshua fell facedown to the ground in reverence, and asked him, "What message does my Lord have for his servant?" The commander of the Lord's army replied, "Take off your sandals, for the place where you are standing is holy." And Joshua did so (Joshua 5:13-15).

JOSHUA saw a man with a sword. Rather than running the other way, he approached him and asked if he was a friend or foe. When the man replied that he was the commander of the army of the Lord, Joshua fell to the ground to honor him. Then immediately he asked if there was a message for him from God. He was willing to do whatever the commander told him.

Points to Ponder

1. When faced with a representative of the Lord, do you give that person the reverence he or she deserves?

2. Are you willing to do whatever the Lord requires of you?

_____

_____

_____

COVENANT VIOLATION

The Lord said to Joshua, "Stand up! What are you doing down on your face? Israel has sinned; they have violated my covenant, which I commanded them to keep. They have taken some of the devoted things; they have stolen, they have lied, they have put them with their own possessions. That is why the Israelites cannot stand against their enemies; they turn their backs and run because they have been made liable to destruction. I will not be with you anymore unless you destroy whatever among you is devoted to destruction (Joshua 7:10-12).

THE Israelites violated God's covenant by stealing and lying. Because of this, God took away His protection. But rather than allowing the Israelites to be destroyed because of their deceit, God makes the problem known to Joshua so he can go to the people and have them destroy the stolen items. God gives us second chances if we are willing to destroy the sin that is possessing us.

Points to Ponder

1. Do you have things in your life that you need to destroy including pride, envy, impatience, vanity, and the like?

2. Do you think He will give you a second chance?

DEATH AND DESTRUCTION

*Then Joshua, together with all Israel, took Achan son of Zerah,
the silver, the robe, the gold wedge, his sons and daughters, his
cattle, donkeys and sheep, his tent and all that he had, to
the Valley of Achor. Joshua said, "Why have you brought this
trouble on us? The Lord will bring trouble on you today." Then
all Israel stoned him, and after they had stoned the rest, they
burned them (Joshua 7:24-25).*

WHEN God is on our side, trouble is on the other side. After
Joshua's encounter with the commander of God's army, he
took the guilty people who had stolen and lied and asked, "Why have
you brought this trouble on us? The Lord will bring trouble on you
today." And sure enough the guilty ones were destroyed along with
the stolen items.

Points to Ponder

1. How serious do you think God is about strict obedience
    to His commands?

2. After reading Joshua 7:25, how serious do you think
    God is about obeying Him?

THE POWER OF A PROPHETIC ACT

Then the Lord said to Joshua, "Hold out toward Ai the javelin that is in your hand, for into your hand I will deliver the city." So Joshua held out toward the city the javelin that was in his hand. As soon as he did this, the men in the ambush rose quickly from their position and rushed forward. They entered the city and captured it..." (Joshua 8:18-19).

A prophetic act or drama is an act or deed or mission inspired by the Holy Spirit to bring or facilitate the agenda of Heaven on earth. It is an enactment of what has happened or exists in the spirit before its physical fulfillment. God gave Joshua the power to overcome a city just by holding out his javelin toward the city—just by obeying God Almighty. That act translated the victory already won in the spirit into the natural world. God has angels waiting in ambush to help you overcome problems and issues that are plaguing you. All you have to do is listen for His command and they will go rushing forward to help you defeat your foes and capture your victory.

Points to Ponder

1. Do you believe that angels are lurking nearby and ready to act upon God's command?
2. Is your javelin in hand, prepared to bring deliverance?

THE SUN AND MOON STOOD STILL

*On the day the Lord gave the Amorites over to Israel, Joshua said to the Lord in the presence of Israel: "Sun, stand still over Gibeon, and you, moon, over the Valley of Aijalon." So **the sun stood still, and the moon stopped, till the nation avenged itself on its enemies,** as it is written in the Book of Jashar. The sun stopped in the middle of the sky and delayed going down about a full day. There has never been a day like it before or since, a day when the Lord listened to a human being. Surely the Lord was fighting for Israel!* (Joshua 10:12-14)

WHAT an amazing and supernatural God orchestrated for Joshua! Of course God can stop the sun and the moon—after all, He created them. He controls every star in every solar system, every ant in every ant hill. Joshua spoke to the Lord in the presence of Israel so the people would know that the Lord their God was the great I Am!

Points to Ponder

1. Do you believe that nothing is impossible for God?
2. Can you fathom the infinite power—and mercy—that God has in every breath that He takes?

THE LORD FOUGHT FOR ISRAEL

Joshua subdued them from Kadesh Barnea to Gaza and from the whole region of Goshen to Gibeon. All these kings and their lands Joshua conquered in one campaign, because ***the Lord, the God of Israel, fought for Israel*** *(Joshua 10:41-42).*

THE Lord fought for Israel and He fights for us today. We can depend on Him to fight our battles for us because He has done so in the past. The Old Testament proves His desire to not only fight for us—but to win our battles. Your enemies will be subdued, not just here and there but the entire region will be conquered in one fell swoop of God's hand.

Points to Ponder

1. Do you sometimes think that you can fight your own battles?

2. Would you rather not bother God with what you consider a small matter?

THE LORD SAVES

He said to David, "Am I a dog, that you come at me with sticks?"
And the Philistine cursed David by his gods. "Come here," he
said, "and I'll give your flesh to the birds and the wild animals!"
David said to the Philistine, "You come against me with sword
and spear and javelin, but I come against you in the name of the
Lord Almighty, the God of the armies of Israel, whom you have
defied. This day the Lord will deliver you into my hands, and I'll
strike you down and cut off your head. This very day I will give
the carcasses of the Philistine army to the birds and the wild
animals, and the whole world will know that there is a God in
Israel. All those gathered here will know that it is not by sword or
spear that the Lord saves; for the battle is the Lord's and he will
give all of you into our hands" (1 Samuel 17:43-47).

GOLIATH came out against the God of Israel, but when David, a
young man at the time, came out empowered by the Lord—the
giant was no match.

Points to Ponder

1. Do you feel outnumbered, outmaneuvered, and out of
    touch in certain situations or when encountering cer-
    tain people?

2. Summon the courage of David and stand up against
    every giant!

THE DANGEROUS SPIRIT OF JEALOUSY

*When the victorious Israelite army was returning home after David had killed the Philistine, women from all the towns of Israel came out to meet King Saul. They sang and danced for joy with tambourines and cymbals. This was their song: "Saul has killed his **thousands,** and David his **ten thousands!"** This made Saul very angry. "What's this?" he said. "They credit David with ten thousands and me with only thousands. Next they'll be making him their king!" So from that time on **Saul kept a jealous eye on David** (1 Samuel 18:6-9 NLT).*

G OD chose Saul as king and he did a good job—until jealousy and unjustified anger overtook him. The spirit of jealousy permeated his mind until he was crazy and obsessed. Saul sought to kill David until the Lord had the final say; Saul was laid to permanent rest while David was proclaimed king—just as Saul predicted.

Points to Ponder

1. Have you heard of "self-professing prophecy"?
2. Do you believe that when you speak a word—whether good or bad—it has power to become reality?

STRENGTHEN ME
JUST ONE MORE TIME

*Then Samson prayed to the Lord, "Sovereign LORD, remember me. **Please, God, strengthen me just once more**, and let me with one blow get revenge on the Philistines for my two eyes." Then Samson reached toward the two central pillars on which the temple stood. Bracing himself against them, his right hand on the one and his left hand on the other, Samson said, "Let me die with the Philistines!" Then he pushed with all his might, and down came the temple on the rulers and all the people in it. Thus he killed many more when he died than while he lived* (Judges 16:28-30).

SAMSON is another biblical character who started out with great potential and then gave in to his fleshly desires and pride. But at the end of his life, he prayed that the Lord would help him get revenge and the Lord obliged. So many people, then and now, must learn the hard way that God's way is the only way to avoid pain and eternal damnation. In the midst of Samson's apparently hopeless situation, he humbles himself and cried to God for help and God strengthened and he killed more enemies in his death.

Points to Ponder

1. Do you make a habit of learning lessons the hard way?
2. If you read the true-life stories in the Bible, can you learn lessons the easy way by avoiding their mistakes?

NO OTHER RELATIONSHIPS

...They attacked them with the sword and burned down their city. There was no one to rescue them because they lived a long way from Sidon and had no relationship with anyone else... (Judges 18:27-28).

G OD uses others to help us along life's journey. We must be open to relationships that God may have in store for us—people who may lighten our loads, make us laugh, keep us balanced. Although our ultimate personal relationship is with God, our Father, we have to be aware of others he may bring alongside. Relationships are important to God.

Points to Ponder

1. Do you have a lot of friends or acquaintances?
2. Are you a "social butterfly" or a private person?
3. Do you shut people out or welcome them into your continually expanding circle of friends?

WORSHIP AS AN ACT OF WARFARE

*While Samuel was sacrificing the burnt offering, the Philistines drew near to engage Israel in battle. But that day **the Lord thundered with loud thunder against the Philistines and threw them into such a panic** that they were routed before the Israelites. The men of Israel rushed out of Mizpah and pursued the Philistines, slaughtering them along the way to a point below Beth Car* (1 Samuel 7:10-11).

A S Israelites offered the burnt sacrifice, the Lord thundered against their enemies and sent panic to the enemy's camp. The Lord is capable of thundering against your enemies even when you are offering a sacrifice of praise and worship to Him. Although we may not face physical danger from our enemies, there are many around the world who are facing torture for their Christian beliefs. Please keep brothers and sisters in Christ in prayer for safety and protection as they defend their faith in Jesus Christ, God's only Son, our Lord.

Points to Ponder

1. Are you routinely offering a sacrifice of praise and worship so your enemies will be thrown into a panic and rooted out from trying to ensnare you?

2. Would you please keep persecuted Christians in your daily prayers?

PREDESTINED FOR THE KINGDOM

In him we were also chosen, having been predestined according to the plan of him who works out everything in conformity with the purpose of his will, in order that we, who were the first to put our hope in Christ, might be for the praise of his glory. And you also were included in Christ when you heard the message of truth, the gospel of your salvation. When you believed, you were marked in him with a seal, the promised Holy Spirit, who is a deposit guaranteeing our inheritance until the redemption of those who are God's possession—to the praise of his glory (Ephesians 1:11-14).

ACCORDING to Paul who was writing to the Ephesians, we have been predestined to conform to God's purpose of His will. We have been included in Christ's glory and have the hope of salvation because we believe His message of truth. The Holy Spirit guarantees our inheritance in God's Kingdom. Hallelujah!

Points to Ponder

1. Have you accepted the gift of salvation and the promise of eternal life with Him?

2. Why or why not?

ENCOURAGING WORDS

*Blessed be the God and Father of our Lord Jesus Christ, who has **blessed us with every spiritual blessing in the heavenly places** in Christ, just as **He chose us** in Him before the foundation of the world, that we should be **holy and without blame before Him in love**, having predestined us to adoption as sons* [and daughters] *by Jesus Christ to Himself, according to the good pleasure of His will, to the praise of the glory of His grace, by which **He made us accepted in the Beloved*** (Ephesians 1:3-6 NKJV).

THESE are encouraging words indeed! God has blessed us (already!) with every spiritual blessing; He chose us; we are holy and without blame; we are His children; and we are accepted! Paul was motivating the church in Ephesus to become Christ-like, to become all that the good Lord intended for them.

Points to Ponder

1. Are you encouraged by these words in Ephesians 1?
2. Can you get excited about your adoption by your heavenly Father and enjoy the glory of His grace?

No Boasting Permitted

*For **by grace you have been saved through faith**, and that not of yourselves; it is the gift of God, not of works, lest anyone should boast. For we are His workmanship, created in Christ Jesus for good works, which God prepared beforehand that we should walk in them (Ephesians 2:8-10 NKJV).*

THERE is nothing we can do to earn salvation. Only by the grace of God have we been saved—it is a gift from God. Although we are destined to help others because that is our gift of love, all we have to do is accept His salvation gift after repenting of our sins and acknowledging Jesus as God's only Son.

Points to Ponder

1. Do you know of believers who like to brag about their "work for the Lord"?
2. Is this spiritual boasting?
3. Do you know believers who work quietly behind the scenes to accomplish God's will?

WALK WORTHY

*I, therefore, the prisoner of the Lord, beseech you to **walk worthy** of the calling with which you were called, with all lowliness and gentleness, with longsuffering, bearing with one another in love, endeavoring to keep the unity of the Spirit in the bond of peace. There is **one body and one Spirit**, just as you were called in one hope of your calling; **one Lord, one faith, one baptism; one God and Father** of all, who is above all, and through all, and in you all* (Ephesians 4:1-6 NKJV).

P AUL is asking the church members in Ephesus to walk worthy of their calling. He is asking them to be kind and gentle, patient and loving. If he had to ask them, it seems they may have been some contention within the church. He calls for unity of the Spirit and a bond of peace. Is your local church united with a bond of peace?

Points to Ponder

1. Are you a prisoner of the Lord?
2. Are you one with the Lord?
3. Do you believe there is one faith and one baptism?

MATURING IN FAITH

*Then we will no longer be infants, tossed back and forth by the waves, and blown here and there by every wind of teaching and by the cunning and craftiness of people in their deceitful scheming. Instead, **speaking the truth in love**, we will grow to become in every respect the mature body of him who is the head, that is, Christ. From him the whole body, joined and held together by every supporting ligament, grows and **builds itself up in love, as each part does its work*** (Ephesians 4:14-16).

CHRISTIANS need to mature in the faith, otherwise they are tossed around in teachings that come from shysters. We have to be sure of what we believe; relying on the Holy Spirit and the word of God for direction. The more we mature, the more we grow to become like Christ.

Points to Ponder

1. Are you older spiritually today than you were last year?
2. Last month?
3. Last week?

PUT OFF FALSEHOOD

*Therefore each of you must **put off falsehood and speak truthfully** to your neighbor, for we are all members of one body. "In your anger **do not sin"**: **Do not let the sun go down while you are still angry,** and **do not give the devil a foothold.** Anyone who has been stealing must **steal no longer,** but must **work,** doing something useful with their own hands, that they may have something to **share with those in need** (Ephesians 4:25-28).*

THERE are several direct admonitions in this passage from Ephesians. Paul is speaking candidly to the church so that no one will misunderstand what he is trying to say. Obviously there were problems in the church that needed to be solved and he was the one God chose to set the people straight.

Points to Ponder

1. Did you feel any sense of conviction as you read this passage?
2. Will you prayerfully consider each of the cautions and vow to obey his advice?

GET RID OF ALL...

Do not let any unwholesome talk come out of your mouths,
*but only what is helpful for **building others up** according*
*to their needs, that it may benefit those who listen. And **do***
***not grieve the Holy Spirit of God**, with whom you were*
*sealed for the day of redemption. **Get rid of all bitterness,***
***rage and anger, brawling and slander**, along with every*
*form of malice. **Be kind and compassionate** to one another,*
***forgiving** each other, just as in Christ God forgave you*
(Ephesians 4:29-32).

A GAIN Paul is admonishing the church. He is telling them how Christians are supposed to live together. First he tells them what not to do: no crude speech; no grieving the Holy Spirit; no bitterness, rage, anger, fighting, lying, or cruelty. Then he tells them what they should do: build others up with helpful words; be kind, compassionate, and forgiving. This isn't the only church he had to bring to task.

Points to Ponder

1. Are you aware of a church that is plagued with these types of issues?
2. If church members are behaving badly, how should the situation handled?

GOD'S WRATH

*But among you there must **not be even a hint of sexual immorality**, or of any kind of **impurity, or of greed**, because these are **improper** for God's holy people. **Nor should there be obscenity, foolish talk or coarse joking**, which are out of place, **but rather thanksgiving**. For of this you can be sure: **No immoral, impure or greedy person—such a person is an idolater—has any inheritance in the kingdom of Christ and of God. Let no one deceive you** with empty words, for because of such **things God's wrath comes on those who are disobedient**. Therefore do not be partners with them* (Ephesians 5:3-7).

IN one of Paul's most powerful discussions about behavior, here in Ephesians 5, he clearly states that we must not be part of sexual immorality, obscenity, dirty jokes, greed, or idolatry. He cautions that God's wrath will be felt by those who engage in these types of activities. We must obey God when it comes to this behavior because they affect not only ourselves but God's reputation, as we are representatives of His Kingdom.

Point to Ponder

1. If you are guilty of these abominations, will you take action today to stop, ask for forgiveness, and repent?

FEARLESSLY DECLARING THE GOSPEL

*And **pray in the Spirit** on all occasions with all kinds of prayers and requests. With this in mind, **be alert and always keep on praying** for all the Lord's people. Pray also for me, that whenever I speak, words may be given me so that I will **fearlessly make known the mystery of the gospel,** for which I am an **ambassador in chains.** Pray that I may declare it **fearlessly,** as I should* (Ephesians 6:18-20).

I N closing his correspondence to the Ephesians, Paul tells the people to pray in the Spirit, to be alert, and to pray for all of God's people. He considers himself an ambassador in chains for Christ and prays that he can share the gospel fearlessly. Paul is a terrific role model for Christians who want to mature and grow their faith.

Points to Ponder

1. What do you think Paul meant when we referred to himself as "an ambassador in chains"?
2. Are you fearless when sharing the gospel?
3. Are you an ambassador in chains?

Reading the Bible in a Year: Psalm 22-24 and Acts 20-1:16.

THE GOAL IS LOVE

*The **goal of this command is love,** which comes from a **pure heart** and a **good conscience** and a **sincere faith.** Some have departed from these and have turned to meaningless talk. They want to be teachers of the law, but they do not know what they are talking about or what they so confidently affirm* (1 Timothy 1:5-7).

THIS passage from First Timothy confirms how timeless the Bible really is. Centuries ago Paul was writing to Timothy about issues that continue to infect our churches today. Many of today's pastors are ramble on and on about meaningless issues and teach laws that have been replaced with the blood of Jesus—yet they are confident about themselves and their beliefs.

Points to Ponder

1. Have you been exposed to pastors or church leaders who fall into this category?
2. How did their preaching or teaching make you feel?

Mercy! I was shown mercy

I thank Christ Jesus our Lord, who has given me strength, that he considered me trustworthy, appointing me to his service. Even though I was once a blasphemer and a persecutor and a violent man, I was shown mercy because I acted in ignorance and unbelief. The grace of our Lord was poured out on me abundantly, along with the faith and love that are in Christ Jesus (1 Timothy 1:12-14).

P AUL wrote to Timothy that before he became a believer, he was a violent persecutor of Christians. But God showed him mercy and grace and consequently he shares the faith and love that Christ Jesus brought to the world. Jesus gave Paul strength and He will give you strength as well to move forward in service to the Lord and toward the abundant life you can live—because of the sacrifice Jesus offered for all upon the cross.

Points to Ponder

1. Were you once a blasphemer and persecutor of Christians?
2. In your ignorance and unbelief did you do or say things that you regret?
3. Have you asked for forgiveness?

_____

_____

_____

PRAYERS FOR LEADERSHIP

*I urge, then, **first of all, that petitions, prayers, intercession and thanksgiving be made for all people**—for kings and all those in authority, that we may **live peaceful and quiet lives in all godliness and holiness**. This is good, and pleases **God our Savior, who wants all people to be saved and to come to a knowledge of the truth**. For there is one God and one mediator between God and mankind, the man Christ Jesus, who gave himself as a ransom for all people...* (1 Timothy 2:1-6).

E VERY Christian should pray for the leaders of their nations. Whether good or bad, leaders need our prayers because of the enormous responsibilities. Pray that they will seek godly wisdom before every decision. Pray that they will make peace a priority. Pray that they will treat the people of their country with compassion and justice. Paul urged Timothy to petition, pray, intercede, and give thanks for those in authority—we should follow suit.

Points to Ponder

1. Have you been routinely praying for the president, prime minister, or other leaders in your country?

2. Do you think there will ever be a time when the world will live in harmony?

JESUS, JESUS, JESUS

Beyond all question, the mystery from which true godliness springs is great: He appeared in the flesh, was vindicated by the Spirit, was seen by angels, was preached among the nations, was believed on in the world, was taken up in glory (1 Timothy 3:16).

J ESUS is the mystery from which true godliness springs. Jesus left His heavenly home to come to earth to redeem a people God loves unconditionally. Jesus was born of a virgin, suffered under Pilate, was crucified, died, and was buried. But! Jesus rose from the grave and sits on the right hand of God the Father. Hallelujah!

Points to Ponder

1. Does your congregation recite the Apostle's Creed regularly in church?
2. If yes, do you repeat the words from memory—or from the heart?

EVERYTHING GOD CREATED IS GOOD

*The Spirit clearly says that in later times some will abandon the faith and follow deceiving spirits and things taught by demons. Such teachings come through hypocritical liars, whose consciences have been seared as with a hot iron. They forbid people to marry and order them to abstain from certain foods, which God created to be received with thanksgiving by those who believe and who know the truth. For **everything God created is good**, and **nothing is to be rejected if it is received with thanksgiving**, because **it is consecrated by the word of Go**d and prayer* (1 Timothy 4:1-5).

O VER the centuries there have been deceiving spirits and demons. Even today there are those who don't know the truth yet impose laws that restrict people from enjoying the freedom that Jesus came to offer. We must not abandon the faith to follow evilness. Use your God-given discernment abilities to reveal the hypocritical liars—and stay far away from them. Reject not gifts from God, thanking Him for His goodness.

Points to Ponder

1. Have you been ensnared by someone who was trying to deceive you about the word of God?

2. Have you been approached by those who say they have a "better way"?

_____

_____

Have Nothing to do with Such People

But mark this: There will be terrible times in the last days. **People will be lovers of themselves, lovers of money, boastful, proud, abusive, disobedient to their parents, ungrateful, unholy, without love, unforgiving, slanderous, without self-control, brutal, not lovers of the good, treacherous, rash, conceited, lovers of pleasure rather than lovers of God—having a form of godliness but denying its power. Have nothing to do with such people** (2 Timothy 3:1-5).

THIS is a comprehensive list of what the last days will look like regarding to people's lifestyle and behavior. Many of these issues are prevalent today. Many of these issues have even infiltrated the church. Although Christians are to go into all the world to preach the gospel, we are to have "nothing to do with such people."

Points to Ponder

1. Do you believe that the existence of these ways of living indicate that we are presently in the "last days"?
2. Do you have relationships with these types of people?

WITH GENTLENESS AND RESPECT

*Who is going to harm you if you are eager to do good? But
even if you should suffer for what is right, you are blessed. "Do
not fear their threats; do not be frightened." But in your hearts
revere Christ as Lord. Always be prepared to give an answer
to everyone who asks you to give the reason for the hope that
you have. But do this with gentleness and respect, keeping a
clear conscience, so that those who speak maliciously against
your good behavior in Christ may be ashamed of their slander*
(1 Peter 3:13-16).

A S believers, we need to be eager to do good; we need to be willing
to suffer for Christ knowing that we will ultimately be blessed;
we are not to fear or be frightened; we must revere Christ as Lord.
We must also be prepared to answer people when they ask about our
heavenly and loving Father. And as believers, we have to be considerate of others, treating them with respect.

Points to Ponder

1. Do you fear threats from those who don't have the same
    beliefs?

2. Can you be respectful when sharing your faith?

3. When you lay your head down at night, is your con-
    science clear from a living a day full of God's goodness?

THE LORD IS OUR SHEPHERD

The Lord is my shepherd, I lack nothing. He makes me lie down in green pastures, he leads me beside quiet waters, he refreshes my soul. He guides me along the right paths for his name's sake. Even though I walk through the darkest valley, I will fear no evil, for you are with me; your rod and your staff, they comfort me (Psalm 23:1-4).

THIS well-known psalm has brought comfort and peace to many Christians during times of grief, sickness, discouragement, and sorrow. He treats us like sheep, lovingly providing all that we need; He soothes our soul with refreshing water; He guides us in the right direction throughout life. And if we walk through dark valleys, we have no reason to fear because we know the Lord is with us. What a promise!

Points to Ponder

1. Have you turned to this psalm during times of distress?
2. What is your favorite verse? Why?

_____

_____

_____

GOODNESS AND LOVE

You prepare a table before me in the presence of my enemies. You anoint my head with oil; my cup overflows. **Surely your goodness and love will follow me all the days of my life,** *and I will dwell in the house of the Lord forever* (Psalm 23:5-6).

CONTINUING with this beloved psalm, we see that the Lord is ready to give us strength before our enemies, He is going to anoint us with His goodness and love, and we will live with Him forever in His house.

Points to Ponder

1. Do the words of this psalm bring peace to your heart?
2. What do these two verses mean to you?

SHOUT FOR JOY

Shout for joy to the Lord, all the earth. Worship the Lord with gladness; come before him with joyful songs. Know that the Lord is God. It is he who made us, and we are his; we are his people, the sheep of his pasture. Enter his gates with thanksgiving and his courts with praise; give thanks to him and praise his name. For the Lord is good and his love endures forever; his faithfulness continues through all generations (Psalm 100:1-5).

WE don't have to be meek and mild as Christians. We can *"shout for joy to the Lord"*; we can *"come before Him with joyful songs"*! I encourage you to boldly enter His gates and courts with thanksgiving and praise. After all, the Lord is good and His love endures forever. Hallelujah!

Points to Ponder

1. Would you be comfortable shouting with joy to the Lord?

2. Can you show your gladness out loud?

3. What is your favorite way to praise and thank Him?

OBEDIENCE BRINGS DIVINE STRENGTH

Observe [obey] *therefore all the commands I am giving you today, so that you may have the strength to go in and take over the land that you are crossing the Jordan to possess, and so that you may live long in the land that the Lord swore to your forefathers to give to them and their descendants, a land flowing with milk and honey* (Deuteronomy 11:8-9).

WHEN you obey God's commands, you will gain strength to face and defeat challenges and possess the victory. You will also live long in a good place, a place where blessings will overflow.

Points to Ponder

1. How are you at obeying God's commands?
2. Are you quick to follow through?
3. Do you plan a course of action?
4. Do you wait and see if God really means it?

SOLOMON'S WILLFUL SIN

The king, moreover, must not acquire great numbers of horses
for himself or make the people return to Egypt to get more of
them, for the Lord has told you, "You are not to go back that
way again." He must not take many wives, or his heart will be
led astray. He must not accumulate large amounts of silver
and gold (Deuteronomy 17:16-17).

SOLOMON indeed did take many wives and his heart was indeed led astray. Even with all that God gave Solomon, including wisdom, Solomon still disobeyed. Was his flesh so overpowering that he couldn't resist temptation? His father David was also tempted and gave in to sexual temptation. Notice a trend in this story. You must stand against any evil trend in your bloodline. Your posterity will not be besieged by the sin that so easily besieges you.

Points to Ponder

1. Why is it so hard to obey God's commands?
2. What causes a person to disregard right and rather choose to do wrong?

_____

_____

_____

OBEDIENCE IS BETTER THAN SACRIFICE

Does the Lord delight in burnt offerings and sacrifices as much as in obeying the Lord? **To obey is better than sacrifice**, *and to heed is better than the fat of rams. For rebellion is like the sin of divination, and arrogance like the evil of idolatry. Because you have rejected the word of the Lord, he has rejected you as king* (1 Samuel 15:22-23).

CLEARLY the Lord delights in obedience. When we rebel against Him and His word, He will reject us. Thankfully, through Jesus we can ask for forgiveness and be restored into His loving arms. The Lord would rather you obey Him than give Him a million sacrifices!

Points to Ponder

1. Are you naturally rebellious or arrogant?
2. Are you naturally compliant and obedient?

REGRET OVER DECISIONS

Until the day Samuel died, he did not go to see Saul again, though Samuel mourned for him. And the Lord regretted [was grieved] that he had made Saul king over Israel (1 Samuel 15:35).

GOD regretted that He had made Saul king over Israel. And Samuel mourned Saul's rejection of righteousness, as he had been the one to anoint Saul. Saul didn't turn out the way the Lord and Samuel thought he would. Sometimes people we know—family, co-workers, church friends—disappoint us. We can stand by them, but we can't allow their actions to affect our relationship with the Lord. Samuel mourned for Saul, that is to say he had pity for how things turned out for Saul; nevertheless, he refused to set his eyes on Saul again! Samuel did not allow his emotions to interfere with his spiritual conviction.

Points to Ponder

1. Were you surprised to read that God could regret or grieve over a decision He made?

2. How often do you grieve over your decisions?

3. Are you grieving for a rebellious loved one?

FIVE-DAY PRAYER AND FASTING
DAY ONE

FOR the next five days, I encourage you to fast—sacrifice—something you enjoy to show your devotion to God. Today's Scripture focus to pray over: *"Oh, that men would give thanks to the Lord for His goodness, and for His wonderful works to the children of men! For He has broken the gates of bronze, and cut the bars of iron in two"* (Psalm 107:15-16). May we break out of all self-imposed limitations and artificial boundaries.

Points to Ponder

1.   What are you going to fast from?
2.   Why is this fast special to you?
3.   What does this Scripture passage mean to you?

_____

_____

_____

FIVE-DAY PRAYER AND FASTING
DAY TWO

F OR the next four days, I encourage you to fast—sacrifice—something you enjoy to show your devotion to God. Today's Scripture focus to pray over: *"There is a river whose streams make glad the city of God, the holy place where the Most High dwells. God is within her, she will not fall; God will help her at break of day"* (Psalm 46:4-5). Living water will flow out of you. You will not fail!

Points to Ponder

1. What are you going to fast from?
2. Why is this fast special to you?
3. What does this Scripture passage mean to you?

Five-Day Prayer and Fasting
Day Three

FOR the next three days, I encourage you to fast—sacrifice—something you enjoy to show your devotion to God. Today's Scripture focus to pray over: *"Let no one be found among you who sacrifices their son or daughter in the fire, who practices divination or sorcery, interprets omens, engages in witchcraft"* (Deuteronomy 18:10). Break the hold of evil spirits through the power of the Holy Spirit in you.

Points to Ponder

1.   What are you going to fast from?
2.   Why is this fast special to you?
3.   What does this Scripture passage mean to you?

FIVE-DAY PRAYER AND FASTING
DAY FOUR

FOR the next two days, I encourage you to fast—sacrifice—something you enjoy to show your devotion to God. Today's Scripture focus to pray over: *"They spoke against God; they said, "Can God really spread a table in the wilderness?"* (Psalm 78:19). Yes! The Lord can provide nourishment for you in any dry and dusty circumstance.

Points to Ponder

1. What are you going to fast from?
2. Why is this fast special to you?
3. What does this Scripture passage mean to you?

Five-Day Prayer and Fasting
Day Five

TODAY, I encourage you to fast—sacrifice—something you enjoy to show your devotion to God. Today's Scripture focus to pray over: *"Who will rise up for me against the wicked? Who will take a stand for me against evildoers? Unless the Lord had given me help, I would soon have dwelt in the silence of death. When I said, "My foot is slipping," your unfailing love, Lord, supported me"* (Psalm 94:16-18; Psalm 106:30-31). May you always stand up for God and against the wicked!

Points to Ponder

1. What are you going to fast from?
2. Why is this fast special to you?
3. What does this Scripture passage mean to you?

ETERNAL VINDICATION

"no weapon forged against you will prevail, and you will refute every tongue that accuses you. This is the heritage of the servants of the Lord, and this is their vindication from me," declares the Lord (Isaiah 54:17).

WHEN people are throwing stones and words at you unjustly, know that the Lord is nearby; He will protect you; he will vindicate you from lies and evilness. The Lord told this truth to Isaiah and this truth remains today for us to lean on, take comfort in, and to lift us up in faith.

Points to Ponder

1. Have you been a victim of vicious, untrue attacks?
2. Have people said lies about you or your family?
3. God will turn all of the attacks away from you—do you believe He is more than capable of vindicating you?

GOD WATCHES OVER YOU

...God watched over me, When His lamp shone above and upon my head and by His light I walked through darkness; as I was in the [prime] ripeness of my days, when the friendship and counsel of God were over my tent, when the Almighty was yet with me and my children were about me, when my steps [through rich pasturage] were washed with butter and the rock poured out for me streams of oil! (Job 29:2-6 AMP)

GOD is always watching over you. He shines His bright light over and before you as you walk through darkness. His friendship and counsel is yours for the asking. Even as you mature and family relationships change, He is faithful to stay with you. He knows your every step along the journey of life.

Points to Ponder

1.   As you look back over your life, can you see God's presence?
2.   Did you feel Him nudging you along through tough times?
3.   Was He there rejoicing with you during good times?

EACH WILL GIVE ACCOUNT

So then, each of us will give an account of ourselves to God
(Romans 14:12)

E ACH of us will give an account to God of our lives. He gifted us with life and we are to use it to His glory. Our lives are more than living day to day going to work or school, watching television, then going to bed. We need to dedicate each day to Him and allow Him to use us to fulfill His will. Pray as such each morning, then at work and at school, listen to His voice telling you what to say, how to act, who to encourage.

Points to Ponder

1. Do you devote a portion of each day to God?
2. Do you pray throughout the day that He will use you?
3. When you give your account to God, will He be pleased?

GOD IS THE JUDGE

Who are you to judge someone else's servant? To their own master, they stand or fall. And they will stand, for the Lord is able to make them stand (Romans 14:4).

GOD is the Judge. We are not to judge others, because much of the time we have as many faults as everyone else. When you are tempted to judge people for something they did or said, turn that thought inward and see if you have ever been guilty of the same action. Rather than judging—try praying.

Points to Ponder

1. Do you know someone who is judgmental? Someone who judges others on their appearance, intelligence, mannerisms?

2. What is your response to people who are judging others unjustly?

_____

_____

_____

GOOD IS GOOD

Do not let what you know is good be spoken of as evil
(Romans 14:16).

WHEN you have a word from the Lord, or the Holy Spirit has spoken a truth from the Bible to you, accept that as good and true. Keep that good word in your heart and absorb it into your spirit. If someone tries to dispute that truth, do not allow it. Stand up for what you know to be good—don't let someone speak of it as evil.

Points to Ponder

1. Have people tried to talk you out of believing what you know is true and good?
2. Can others sway you from standing on God's word to you?

JESUS—THE SAME FOREVER

Jesus Christ is the same yesterday and today and forever
(Hebrews 13:8).

J ESUS never changes. His love for us has been the same over every
century. Unlike the world where people change their minds, loving and unloving with a blow of the wind, Jesus' unconditional love
endures forever.

Points to Ponder

1. How committed are you to the people you love?
2. Do you love them unconditionally?
3. Or do you have some stipulations or standards to which
   they must conform?

A Love So Deep

*See what **great love the Father has lavished on us**, that we should be called children of God! And that is what we are! The reason the world does not know us is that it did not know him. Dear friends, now **we are children of God**, and what we will be has not yet been made known. But we know that when Christ appears, we shall be like him, for we shall see him as he is. All who have this hope in him purify themselves, just as he is pure* (1 John 3:1-3).

WE are God's children. He lavishes us with His great love—every day, every moment. His love is beyond our comprehension. If the world rejects us, it is because people don't recognize His love in us. Therefore, we must try our best to portray His love to them—bring them into the family of God.

Points to Ponder

1. Does your lifestyle reflect your place in God's family?
2. Why or why not?

HOPE SPRINGS ETERNAL

And hope does not put us to shame, because God's love has been poured out into our hearts through the Holy Spirit, who has been given to us (Romans 5:5).

H OPE is life to many people who are down and out. When people have hope for a better day, a healing, a job, or a relationship restoration, it gives them strength and motivation to go on. Giving hope to others encourages them to face another day where their hope may be realized. God's love poured into our hearts through the Holy Spirit brings eternal hope.

Point to Ponder

1. Have you ever been shamed by others for the hope you have?

_____

_____

_____

BORN OF GOD

*Yet to all who did receive him, to **those who believed** in his name, he gave the right to become **children of God**—children born not of natural descent, nor of human decision or a husband's will, but **born of God** (John 1:12-13).*

PEOPLE who believe in God and glorify His name become His children. He is not a tyrannical father who berates His children, abuses them, or ignores them. God the Father is loving, merciful, and ever-present.

Points to Ponder

1. Are you born of God?
2. Have you accepted His offer of adoption into His family?
3. Do you welcome Him as your Father?

FALSE TEACHINGS

Do not be carried about by different and varied and alien teachings; for it is good for the heart to be established and ennobled and strengthened by means of grace (God's favor and spiritual blessing) and not [to be devoted to] foods [rules of diet and ritualistic meals], which bring no [spiritual] benefit or profit to those who observe them (Hebrews 13:9 AMP).

SOME in the church have peculiar thoughts about foods, diets, and ritualistic meals. We must be discerning of these teachings. Ask God about anything you hear that doesn't sound right or seems to be contrary to His word.

Points to Ponder

1. Are you careful not to accept every word that is offered to you?
2. Are you careful not to "carried about by different and varied and alien teachings"?

ASK GOD

If any of you lacks wisdom, you should ask God, who gives generously to all without finding fault, and it will be given to you (James 1:5).

TO know what to do, ask God. James tells us that if we lack wisdom, we should ask God and He will give us the wisdom we need. We may need wisdom about a teaching we heard, about a financial issue, about a family dispute, about a situation at work. Anytime we don't know what to do, or lack wisdom, if we ask God, He will provide the wisdom we need.

Point to Ponder

1. Do you routinely seek God's wisdom when faced with problems or decisions to make?

ACCEPTABLE RELIGION

Religion that God our Father accepts as pure and faultless is this: to look after orphans and widows in their distress and to keep oneself from being polluted by the world (James 1:27).

R ELIGIONS of all sorts have risen around the world. Members of each religion believe that theirs is the only true religion. What does God have to say about religion? He says that the only pure and faultless religion is one that looks after orphans and widows and the people keep themselves from being polluted by the world. This is the gospel of Christ. Is that the religion you belong to?

Points to Ponder

1. Has your religion become polluted by the world?
2. Is your religion committed to providing for orphans and widows?

TAKE ACTION

Do not merely listen to the word, and so deceive yourselves.
Do what it says (James 1:22).

MANY people listen to Scriptures being read in church every week, or maybe twice a week. But putting God's word into action keeps us from deceiving ourselves—thinking that we are righteous. We must go out into the world to especially care for children and single mothers. James tells us to *"Do what it says"*—to put our faith in action.

Points to Ponder

1. Are you an active or passive Christian?
2. Are there opportunities in your church or neighborhood for you to take advantage of to help others?

SHOW NO FAVORITISM

My brothers and sisters, believers in our glorious Lord Jesus Christ, must not show favoritism (James 2:1).

A S believers in Jesus Christ, we are to show no favoritism when interacting with others. God is our perfect example, as He loves each and every person He created. When Jesus walked the earth, He spoke to and ate with and associated with people of all nationalities and ethnicities; His disciples were from all walks of life. He treated each person as special creations of God.

Points to Ponder

1. Is it sometimes hard for you to accept people who look or talk or act different from you?
2. Can you see people through the eyes of God's love?

LIFELESS

*For as the human body apart from the spirit is lifeless, so
faith apart from [its] works of obedience is also dead*
(James 2:26 AMP).

WITHOUT the Spirit within us, we are dead. Without deeds done in God's name, our faith is dead.

Points to Ponder

1. How Spirit-filled are you?
2. Do you daily pray for a fresh infilling of the Holy Spirit?

FAITH MADE COMPLETE

*You see that his faith and his actions were working together,
and his faith was made complete by what he did* (James 2:22).

FAITH is made complete by what you do for the Kingdom. Although we can't "earn" salvation, God does expect us, as a natural next step after accepting Jesus as Lord and Savior, to want to help advance His work in the world. Spreading the good news of the gospel includes being good examples of His love and mercy—at home, at work, at school, in the marketplace.

Points to Ponder

1. Is your faith being continually made complete by putting your faith in action?

2. Are you a good example of someone who has faith in Jesus?

A CONSUMING FORCE

For the Lord your God is a consuming fire, a jealous God
(Deuteronomy 4:24).

OUR God is a consuming fire, or force. He is jealous of us and wants our full attention, love, and devotion. Have you ever been near a raging fire? The power of it can be overwhelming. God's jealousy is like that raging fire—He loves and wants you that much.

Points to Ponder

1. Are you willing to allow His fire to consume you totally?
2. Can you fully give yourself over to your jealous heavenly Father?

BURN YOUR IDOLS

This is what you are to do to them: Break down their altars, smash their sacred stones, cut down their Asherah poles and burn their idols in the fire. For you are a people holy to the Lord your God. The Lord your God has chosen you out of all the peoples on the face of the earth to be his people, his treasured possession (Deuteronomy 7:5-6).

P EOPLE too quickly forget that the Lord is the One who brings them out of slavery and bondage and turmoil. They replace Him with things, with idols of every shape and size. But God is a jealous God and requires that we break down our false altars and burn our deceitful idols. We must follow His commands and turn only to Him to praise and worship.

Points to Ponder

1. Are there idols in your life that need to be destroyed, burnt?

2. Have you erected altars to things, people, or activities other than God that need to be broken down?

WHAT THE LORD REQUIRES

*And now, Israel, what does the Lord your God ask of you
but to fear the Lord your God, to walk in obedience to him,
to love him, to serve the Lord your God with all your heart
and with all your soul, and to observe the Lord's commands
and decrees that I am giving you today for your own good?*
(Deuteronomy 10:12-13)

THROUGHOUT the Bible—Old Testament and New Testament—we are given specific instruction about how to please, honor, worship, and praise God, the Creator of the heavens and earth.

Points to Ponder

1. What does the Lord require of you?
2. Do you fear Him, obey Him, love Him, serve Him, and observe His commands?

_____

_____

_____

THE LORD OF LORDS

For the Lord your God is God of gods and Lord of lords, the great God, mighty and awesome, who shows no partiality and accepts no bribes. He defends the cause of the fatherless and the widow, and loves the foreigner living among you, giving them food and clothing (Deuteronomy 10:17-18).

OUR God is the God of all gods; He is the Lord of lords. As mighty and awesome as He is, He takes special interest in the little children who have no father and the mothers who have no husbands and the people who are displaced. God is so very loving and mindful of the downtrodden. He gives them opportunities to better themselves through His family—us.

Points to Ponder

1. Have you had the opportunity to help those less fortunate?
2. Have you sought out ways to help others?

PROCLAIMING BLESSINGS AND CURSES

When the Lord your God has brought you into the land you are entering to possess, you are to proclaim on Mount Gerizim the blessings, and on Mount Ebal the curses (Deuteronomy 11: 29).

WHEN the Lord brings us into our Promised Land, He will reveal blessings and curses so you will be aware. Share these revelations with others so they will know that your God is the God of blessings—that everyone can access if they turn to the Lord with a contrite heart.

Point to Ponder

1. Do you routinely proclaim God's blessings in your life so that others will see His goodness and mercy?

Forty Years of Daily Provision

Yet the Lord says, "During the forty years that I led you through the wilderness, your clothes did not wear out, nor did the sandals on your feet (Deuteronomy 29:5).

GOD daily provided for the needs of His people while they traveled through the desert to reach the Promised Land. Although they caused the long journey because of their disobedience, God was faithful to sustain them—even making sure that their clothes and sandals didn't wear out.

Points to Ponder

1. Is it reassuring to know that even though you may be disobedient, God will continue to provide for your needs?

2. Do you daily thank Him for His daily provision?

Prosperity

*The Lord your God will put all these curses on your enemies who hate and persecute you. **You will again obey the Lord and follow all his commands I am giving you today.** Then the Lord your **God** will make you most prosperous in all the work of your hands and in the fruit of your womb, the young of your livestock and the crops of your land. **The Lord will again delight in you and make you prosperous,** just as he delighted in your fathers* (Deuteronomy 30:7-9).

GOD wants to delight in us. As we continue to obey Him and follow His directions for our lives, He will make us prosperous. He will bless the work of our hands, our children, our household, and our employment. We must follow all His commands to be assured of prosperity.

Points to Ponder

1. Are you amazed at how much God delights in you?
2. Are you thrilled that He wants to prosper you?
3. Are you willing to obey Him and all of His commands?

HIS WORD

*Now **what I am commanding you today is not too difficult for you or beyond your reach**. It is not up in heaven, so that you have to ask, "Who will ascend into heaven to get it and proclaim it to us so we may **obey it**?" Nor is it beyond the sea, so that you have to ask, "Who will cross the sea to get it and proclaim it to us so we may **obey it**?" No, **the word is very near you**; it is in your mouth and in your heart so you may **obey it*** (Deuteronomy 30:11-14).

HIS word is in our mouth and in our hearts so we may obey it and share it with all who will receive. God doesn't hide His word in Heaven or out in the middle of the ocean—no, His word is within us. His word is part of who we are—if we take the time to hear Him, read the Bible, and absorb His truth.

Points to Ponder

1. Do you obey His word that is in your mouth and in your heart?

2. Do you obey His command that is not too difficult or beyond your reach?

LOVE, LISTEN, HOLD FAST

*and that you may **love the Lord your God, listen to his voice, and hold fast to him. For** the Lord is your life, and he will give you many years in the land he swore to give to your fathers...* (Deuteronomy 30:20).

T HE Lord should totally consume our lives. He is our life—He created us in His likeness. As we love Him and listen to His voice and hold fast to Him, He will give us many years on the earth. Time we can use to advance His Kingdom and His agenda of grace and mercy for all.

Points to Ponder

1. How carefully do you listen for His voice?
2. Do you believe He can speak to you through others, through circumstances, through nature?

GOD-GIVEN SKILLS

Bless all his skills, Lord, and be pleased with the work of his hands. Strike down those who rise against him, his foes till they rise no more (Deuteronomy 33:11).

GOD has blessed each of us with special talents and skills. He will bless those abilities when we use them for His glory. Skills may range from accounting and hair styling to medical and home-making. No matter the work of your hands, when they are used to help others, God will be pleased. He will smite your foes so you can continue to be productive.

Point to Ponder

1. Are you using your God-given talents and skills to benefit others?

THE SPIRIT OF PISGAH
(FAILURE AT THE VERGE OF COMPLETION)

This is the land I promised on oath to Abraham, Isaac and Jacob when I said, "I will give it to your descendants." I have let you see it with your eyes, but you will not cross over into it (Deuteronomy 34:4).

THESE were the words of God to Moses, His servant. At Mount Pisgah, Moses was allowed to see the Promised Land, but God did not permit him to cross over with the Israelites into the land. Anything that wants to stop you when you are close to the completion of your assignment is the spirit of Pisgah—may it not have dominion over you.

Points to Ponder

1. May the spirit of Pisgah not prevail over you and your family.
2. Have you asked for forgiveness for anything that may prevent a godly legacy?

_____

_____

_____

God's Words Are Life

...Take to heart all the words I [Moses] have solemnly declared to you this day, so that you may command your children to obey carefully all the words of this law. They are not just idle words for you—they are your life... (Deuteronomy 32:45-47).

MOSES was the leader of God's chosen people. These chosen people, like us, didn't always obey God's commandments. Moses had to repeatedly remind them how vital it was for them to obey God—for their own benefit. Today, we have our pastor and the Holy Spirit to remind us about keeping our focus on the Lord and His commands.

Points to Ponder

1. Do you remind your children to obey carefully all the words of God?

2. Do you listen carefully for the Holy Spirit's reminders... and reprimands?

LOOK FORWARD

Moses my servant is dead. Now then, you and all these people,
get ready to cross the Jordan River into the land I am about
to give to them—to the Israelites. I will give you every place
where you set your foot, as I promised Moses (Joshua 1:2-3).

WE must look forward—the past is not the future. Looking into the past for too long keeps you from moving forward, to advancing into what the Lord has waiting for you. Moses took the people as far as God allowed. Then the next generation stepped into the land overflowing with blessings for them. They had to move forward into their destiny—as do we.

Points to Ponder

1. Are you stuck in the past?
2. Do you dwell on what happened in the past?
3. What was said in the past?
4. What mistakes you made in the past?

_____

_____

_____

NO ONE WILL
STAND AGAINST YOU

No one will be able to stand against you all the days of your life. As I was with Moses, so I will be with you; I will never leave you nor forsake you (Joshua 1:5).

HOW incredible that God promises that no one will be able to stand against us for as long as we live! His promise to always be with us, never forsaking us is one of the overwhelming truths that makes Christianity so powerful. Jesus doesn't keep track of our sins and then choose whether or not He will love us or leave us. No. He is forever with us.

Points to Ponder

1. Do you depend on God's promise never to leave you or forsake you?

2. Do you believe this with all your heart?

PROSPEROUS AND SUCCESSFUL

Keep this Book of the Law always on your lips; meditate on it day and night, so that you may be careful to do everything written in it. Then you will be prosperous and successful (Joshua 1:8).

JOSHUA 1:8 tells us to keep God's word always on our lips and minds, and to do everything written in it. If we do, we will be prosperous and successful. That sounds easy, doesn't it? Well, some days can be harder than others to be mindful of God's commands. Nevertheless, it benefits us greatly if we remember and obey all of His promises.

Points to Ponder

1. Have you made an effort to memorize Scripture?
2. Why or why not?

DO NOT BE TERRIFIED OR DISCOURAGED

Have I not commanded you? Be strong and courageous. Do not be terrified; do not be discouraged, for the Lord your God will be with you wherever you go (Joshua 1:9).

WE must put our trust in God. Trusting God gives us the strength and courage to forge ahead even when the next steps may bring disaster. We can face disaster and turmoil if we know God is with us wherever we go. Daniel knew God was with him when he faced the hungry lions; David knew God was with him when he faced the murderous giant; Paul knew God was with him when he faced being tossed overboard into a raging sea.

Points to Ponder

1. Do you have the assurance that "God will be with you wherever you go"?

2. Can you face any problem confidently and courageously knowing that He is with you?

HIS WAYS ARE NOT OUR WAYS

Then the Lord said to Joshua, "See, I have delivered Jericho into your hands, along with its king and its fighting men. March around the city once with all the armed men. Do this for six days. Have seven priests carry trumpets of rams' horns in front of the ark. On the seventh day, march around the city seven times, with the priests blowing the trumpets. When you hear them sound a long blast on the trumpets, have all the people give a loud shout; then the wall of the city will collapse and the army will go up, everyone straight in" (Joshua 6:2-5).

HUMAN logic says this type of strategy would not work. Marching around the city and blowing trumpets and then shouting seems ludicrous. But Joshua knew that God's ways are not our ways so he obeyed the Lord and did as commanded. Sure enough, the walls came crashing down and the city was captured.

Points to Ponder

1. Do you question God's ways?
2. Do you wonder if God knows what He is doing?
3. Or do you accept God's methods as higher and better?

Our Inheritance

After Joshua had dismissed the Israelites, they went to take possession of the land, each to their own inheritance
(Judges 2:6).

JOSHUA'S victory for the Lord meant that the people could take possession of the land and each had a portion as their inheritance. Jesus came to repossess the land, which means that we can take possession of Kingdom land. As heirs to His throne through the blood of our Savior, our inheritance is assured.

Points to Ponder

1. What does claiming your Kingdom inheritance mean to you?

2. Have you staked your claim?

A SET-UP FROM THE LORD?

...But Samson said to his father, "Get her for me. She's the right one for me." (His parents did not know that this was from the Lord, who was seeking an occasion to confront the Philistines; for at that time they were ruling over Israel.) (Judges 14:3-4).

Points to Ponder

1. What if this was a set-up from the Lord, a test?
2. What if Samson's father would have refused to get the woman his son wanted?
3. How would you write the rest of Samson's story?

_____

_____

_____

A PROCESSION OF PROPHETS

After that you will go to Gibeah of God, where there is a Philistine outpost. As you approach the town, you will meet a procession of prophets coming down from the high place with lyres, tambourines, flutes and harps being played before them, and they will be prophesying. The Spirit of the Lord will come upon you in power, and you will prophesy with them; and you will be changed into a different person. Once these signs are fulfilled, do whatever your hand finds to do, for God is with you (1 Samuel 10:5-7).

WHAT a sight that must have been! A parade of prophets making music and prophesying. Samuel told these things to Saul who was changed after the Spirit of the Lord came upon him. Saul became a momentary prophet and he was filled with righteousness. Yes, this is the same Saul who later sought to kill David because of the spirit of jealousy that overpowered him. We must be vigilant to allow only the Spirit of the Lord to fill us.

Points to Ponder

1. Has the Spirit of the Lord come upon you in power?
2. Have you been changed into a different person?

 *September 11*

FOR GAINING WISDOM
AND INSTRUCTION

The proverbs of Solomon son of David, king of Israel: for **gaining wisdom and instruction**; *for* **understanding words** *of insight; for* **receiving instruction** *in prudent behavior,* **doing what is right and just and fair**; *for* **giving prudence** *to those who are simple,* **knowledge and discretion** *to the young—let the wise listen and add to their learning, and let the discerning get guidance—for understanding proverbs and parables, the sayings and riddles of the wise* (Proverbs 1:1-6).

S OLOMON wrote the book of Proverbs for several important reasons. Read the passage above again, slowly. Knowing that God
gave Solomon extraordinary wisdom makes this book of the Bible
even more crucial and worth the time to examine more closely.

Points to Ponder

1. Do you have a favorite Proverb?
2. Do any of the Proverbs have special meaning to you?
3. Have you memorized any of the Proverbs?

PARENTS' WISDOM

Listen, my son, to your father's instruction and do not forsake your mother's teaching. They are a garland to grace your head and a chain to adorn your neck (Proverbs 1:8-9).

APPRECIATING our parents and the wisdom they share is beneficial for us. We need to listen to them because they know what is best for us. Respecting them for their position in the family will bring us grace and favor with the Lord.

Points to Ponder

1. Do you believe that you should listen to your father's instruction and not forget your mother's teachings?

2. Why or why not?

September 13

LIVING WITHOUT FEAR OF HARM

*For the waywardness of the simple will kill them, and the
complacency of fools will destroy them; but whoever listens
to me will live in safety and be at ease, without fear of harm*
(Proverbs 1:32-33).

S IMPLE and foolish people are often wayward and complacent.
This makes them targets for evil, which produces fear. But whoever listens and heeds the Lord lives in safety and comfort—with the
fear of harm.

Point to Ponder

1.   Are you simple and foolish or wise and fearless?

_____

_____

_____

WISDOM, UNDERSTANDING, KNOWLEDGE

*By **wisdom** the Lord laid the earth's foundations, by **understanding** he set the heavens in place; by his **knowledge** the watery depths were divided, and the clouds let drop the dew (Proverbs 3:19-20).*

THREE distinct words are used in these verses: wisdom, understanding, and knowledge. Many people use these words interchangeably. According to this passage and the content, each have a unique meaning: wisdom meaning life application of the word of God; understanding meaning true and valued judgement/discernment; and knowledge meaning awareness. May all of these work for you.

Points to Ponder

1. Can you define wisdom? Understanding? Knowledge?
2. Are they different in your mind?

DO NOT WITHHOLD GOOD

Do not withhold good from those to whom it is due, when it is in your power to act. Do not say to your neighbor, "Come back tomorrow and I'll give it to you"—when you already have it with you. Do not plot harm against your neighbor, who lives trustfully near you. Do not accuse anyone for no reason—when they have done you no harm (Proverbs 3:27-30).

EVERYDAY wisdom is contained in this passage from God's word. We should extend our hand in friendship and assistance to those in need, especially neighbors. Most everyone has lived beside a neighbor who hasn't been friendly or helpful or considerate. No matter the infraction, as God's ambassadors, we should not withhold good if we can help in any way.

Points to Ponder

1. Do you need to be reminded about how to be a good neighbor?
2. Have you been frustrated with an inconsiderate neighbor?
3. Have you been an inconsiderate neighbor?

CONTRASTS

For the Lord detests the perverse but takes the upright into his confidence. The Lord's curse is on the house of the wicked, but he blesses the home of the righteous. He mocks proud mockers but shows favor to the humble and oppressed. The wise inherit honor, but fools get only shame (Proverbs 3:32-35).

THESE verses in Proverbs 3 show several contrasts between the perverse and the upright; the wicked and the righteous; the proud and the humble; and the wise and the fool. Much can be learned from these comparisons, and much can be gained by being upright (God's confidant); righteous (blessings); humble (favor); and wise (honor).

Point to Ponder

1. Knowing that the Lord is pleased with upright, right-eous, humble, and wise believers, are you looking forward to being His confidant, having your home blessed, and receiving His favor and honor?

CONSIDER THE ANT

You lazy fool, look at an ant. Watch it closely; let it teach you a thing or two. Nobody has to tell it what to do. All summer it stores up food; at harvest it stockpiles provisions. So how long are you going to laze around doing nothing? How long before you get out of bed? A nap here, a nap there, a day off here, a day off there, sit back, take it easy—do you know what comes next? Just this: You can look forward to a dirt-poor life, poverty your permanent houseguest! (Proverbs 6:6-8 The Message)

THE Message version of this Bible passage uses some stern words for those who are lazy. Even ants works hard to store food and provisions—they don't lay around in bed napping or laze around doing nothing. People need to be productive, to use their skills to make a living, to be a fruitful member of God's Kingdom and the world's society. No one deserves a free ride.

Points to Ponder

1. Do you know people who laze around all day yet expect food on the table each night?

2. Are there people in your circle of influence who are living a dirt-poor life, with poverty as their permanent houseguest?

3. If yes, what can you do to help motivate them?

_____

_____

_____

COMMITMENT TO HIS WORD

*There are **six things the Lord hates, seven that are detestable**
to him: haughty eyes, a lying tongue, hands that shed innocent
blood, a heart that devises wicked schemes, feet that are quick
to rush into evil, a false witness who pours out lies and a person
who stirs up conflict in the community* (Proverbs 6:16-19).

"HATE" and "detestable" are strong words! They should get our
attention and bring focus on the seven things God hates and
detests: arrogance; lying; murder; wicked scheming; taking part in
evil; liars; agitators. May we never be counted among any of these!

Points to Ponder

1. Were you surprised at this list?
2. Would you add anything to the list that is particularly
   heinous in your opinion?

POVERTY AND WEALTH

Lazy hands make for poverty, but diligent hands bring wealth.
He who gathers crops in summer is prudent, but he who sleeps
during harvest is disgraceful (Proverbs 10:4-5 paraphrase).

B ELIEVERS are to set good examples for others who are always watching us. When they see hard workers who are successful because of their diligence, they will believe that the Lord is good and they will want to be like us.

Points to Ponder

1. Are you diligent and hard-working?
2. Are you prudently taking the right steps to move forward in your career?

GIVING AND SELLING

A generous person will prosper; whoever refreshes others will be refreshed. People curse the one who hoards grain, but they pray God's blessing on the one who is willing to sell (Proverbs 11:25-26).

ACCORDING to these verses in Proverbs 11, generous people will prosper by sharing their resources with others; a hoarder will be cursed; and a people who sell their wares will be blessed. There is a time to give and a time to sell. As long as we sell at fair rates, the Lord will bless our business.

Points to Ponder

1. Are you considered by others as a generous person?
2. Are you a hoarder of things that others can use?
3. Do you sell your wares or services for a reasonable price?

FOOLS AND FOOLISHNESS

The way of fools seems right to them, but the wise listen to advice. Fools show their annoyance at once, but the prudent overlook an insult (Proverbs 12:15-16).

FOOLISH people see life the way they want to, they don't ask for advice. Wise people listen to advice and then discern what they have heard. Foolish people are easily offended. Wise people overlook insults and offenses.

Points to Ponder

1. What category do you mostly fall in—foolish or wise?
2. Are you willing to ask for and listen to advice?
3. Are you willing to be more obliging to those who may inadvertently insult you?

HATE WHAT IS FALSE

The righteous hate what is false, but the wicked make themselves
a stench and bring shame on themselves (Proverbs 13:5).

AGAIN, "hate" is a strong word that brings attention to how we, the righteous of the Lord, should consider lies and falsehoods. The wicked welcome untruths if it makes them feel good or gives them a benefit of some kind. This attitude eventually brings only stench and shame on themselves.

Points to Ponder

1. Are you quick to denounce falsehoods?
2. Do you consistently stand for righteousness and justice for all?

A TREE OF LIFE

Hope deferred makes the heart sick, but a longing fulfilled is a tree of life (Proverbs 13:12).

I F we defer our hope of achieving our dreams and destiny, our heart will become sick, which may transfer to our becoming physically ill. Don't be afraid to hope and dream and reach out toward your destiny. God will give you the desires of your heart—just ask and rather than heart-sick, you will be a fruitful tree of life.

Point to Ponder

1. Write down your top three hopes and dreams. Believe that God will show you how to achieve them.

TROUBLE VERSUS REWARDS

Trouble pursues the sinner, but the righteous are rewarded with good things (Proverbs 13:21).

WHEN people are plagued with trouble, it could mean many things. First, it could mean that there is sin in their lives. This is important because it means at least the person can do something about it. It may mean self-checking to look for any sin—seen or unseen—and ask God to uncover whatever they are doing, saying, or thinking that may be causing the trouble. When people are righteous—deliberate about doing the right thing in public *and* private—they are rewarded with good things. Let's be righteous!

Points to Ponder

1. Do you know people who always seem to be in trouble—financial, emotional, relational?

2. Are you such a person?

3. Could there be hidden sin in your life?

NO ONE ELSE

Each heart knows its own bitterness, and no one else can share its joy (Proverbs 14:10).

EVERYONE has their own internal struggles, feelings of inadequacy, bitterness, and failure. Talking to others about such things may bring comfort, but that comfort is only temporary, for *no one else can share its joy.* It is vitally important, for our spiritual, mental, and emotional health, to share your innermost feelings with Jesus—only He can mend broken hearts and destroy bitterness. He is your Mediator with God the Father who shares your every joy.

Points to Ponder

1. Are there feelings that you share with others that you should be sharing only with Jesus?

2. Are there emotions that are overwhelming you that only Jesus can subdue?

Evil Schemes

A quick-tempered person does foolish things, and the one who devises evil schemes is hated (Proverbs 14:17).

I N a previously highlighted proverb, we noticed that God hates ones who devise evil schemes. Here again is mentioned God's hatred for those who hatch evilness against others. It seems that being quick-tempered—hot headed—may be the key to this type of behaviour. If we quickly react rashly to situations, evil can gain a foothold. Let's learn to restrain ourselves so we will be loved by God, not hated.

Points to Ponder

1. Do you have a quick temper?
2. What steps can you take to control your reactions?
3. Is it possible to change this character trait?

ROTTEN BONES

A heart at peace gives life to the body, but envy rots the bones
(Proverbs 14:30).

WHEN people are envious, it affects not only their personality, but it may also cause physical suffering. Envy, left unrepented of, will eat away at people's minds, enlarging the emotion to a bigger-than-healthy matter. God gives to each what we need—controlling our wants is our responsibility. Be pleased for the person who has more than you, appreciate what you have, aspire to gain more by hard work; and above all, trust that God will give you the desires of your heart—in His perfect timing and according to His perfect will for you.

Points to Ponder

1. Are you an envious person?
2. Do you have a heart of peace that energizes your life day in and day out?

HOW MUCH BETTER?

How much better to get wisdom than gold, to get insight rather than silver! (Proverbs 16:16)

HOW much better is it to have wisdom and insight than riches? This verse from Proverbs 16 seems to indicate that it is *much better!* Solomon had riches and wisdom. Yet he fell into sexual temptation and married foreign women against God's command. Did Solomon place more value on his things than God's gift of wisdom and insight?

Points to Ponder

1. Why do you think it is better to have wisdom and insight rather than riches?
2. What does wisdom and insight give you that is better than riches?

_____

_____

_____

PERVERSION AND GOSSIP

A perverse person stirs up conflict, and a gossip separates close friends (Proverbs 16:28).

W ICKED, perverse, people have a penchant for stirring up conflict—within others, families, communities, and at the workplace. People who gossip do the same, including separating close friends. Notice that the proverb says "close friends," meaning that even our dearest friends can leave us because of gossip. Believers are not to be perverse or gossipers.

Points to Ponder

1. Do you know people who are constantly causing turmoil and gossiping about others?
2. How do you handle these types of people?

_____

_____

_____

The Purity of Children

Even small children are known by their actions, so is their conduct really pure and upright? Ears that hear and eyes that see—the Lord has made them both (Proverbs 20:11-12).

THE purity of children is mentioned throughout the Bible. They accept truth without doubt and enjoy love with open arms. Their ears hear directly from the Lord without being filtered through doctrine and dogma; their eyes see Him clearly for who He is.

Point to Ponder

1. How childlike are you when it comes to hearing and seeing your heavenly Father?

SWEET GRAVEL

Food gained by fraud tastes sweet, but one ends up with a mouth full of gravel (Proverbs 20:17).

B ELIEVERS are faced with unscrupulous people every day. There are those who make their living by fraudulent and conniving means. We see them eating, drinking, and being merry, and we may feel a bit envious—but, the Scripture tells us that eventually those people will be eating gravel.

Point to Ponder

1. The next time you feel a bit envious of someone enjoying things gained by dishonesty, will you remember that their mouth is really full of gravel?

HUMILITY'S WAGES

Humility is the fear of the Lord; its wages are riches and honor and life (Proverbs 22:4).

HUMILITY is another word for modesty, meekness, an unassuming nature. Humility in this proverb is associated with *"the fear of the Lord."* Fearing the Lord is revering Him, respecting Him—and in return you will earn and receive riches, honor, and life!

Points to Ponder

1. Do you humbly live in fear of the Lord?
2. Have you earned your wages?

RAISING CHILDREN

Start children off on the way they should go, and even when they are old they will not turn from it (Proverbs 22:6).

THIS verse has been a comfort to many parents of wayward teenagers. If we raise our children to respect and fear the Lord, if we tell them about His goodness and what Jesus did for them, if we show them the tangible blessings that God bestows on those who love Him, then we can rest assured that our children will remember their heavenly Father and return to Him.

Points to Ponder

1. Have you taken comfort in this verse over the years when raising your children?
2. Do you know others who have received hope through this verse?

Arrogance and Haughtiness

Do you see a person wise in their own eyes? There is more hope for a fool than for them (Proverbs 26:12).

A person who is "wise in their own eyes" is arrogant and haughty—the opposite of being humble. Others are turned away from people who think too much of themselves. There is a big difference between being confident and being arrogant, and believers must stay on the side of being confident in the Lord rather than having a haughty spirit.

Points to Ponder

1. Have you been "turned off" by an arrogant person?
2. Have you met arrogant Christians?

FLAMING ARROWS OF DEATH

*Like a maniac shooting flaming arrows of death is one
who deceives their neighbor and says, "I was only joking!"*
(Proverbs 26:18-19).

MANY times people say and do things that they think have no
consequence. On the contrary they may be starting a fire that
brings death to others—piercing their hearts with unkind words, killing their ambitions with insults, stifling love with dirty jokes.

Points to Ponder

1. Are there maniacs living and working around you?
2. Do their flaming arrows of death cause you to slink
    away or stand firmly for what is right and true?

GODLY LEADERS

When a country is rebellious, it has many rulers, but a ruler with discernment and knowledge maintains order. A ruler who oppresses the poor is like a driving rain that leaves no crops (Proverbs 28:2-3).

THERE is chaos worldwide these days. Countries are in turmoil over politicians, economics, and religion. People are becoming rebellious because the rulers seem to have no discernment and knowledge of right and wrong. The poor are being oppressed and there seems to be no hope in sight. Believers must pray for good leaders who will lift up the people and do what is right.

Points to Ponder

1. Are you worried about the spiritual and economic condition of your country?
2. Are you daily praying for godly men and women to be raised up and put into positions of leadership?

ROLE MODELS

Whoever leads the upright along an evil path will fall into their own trap, but the blameless will receive a good inheritance (Proverbs 28:10).

A S children of God we are to be good examples, role models, of His mercy and grace. We are to help others come to know the saving love and sacrifice of Christ Jesus. Those who don't know the Lord are watching how we react, listening to what we say, wondering what we think. We need to be reacting in love, speaking God's truth, and thinking about others.

Points to Ponder

1. Do you consider yourself a good example of God's mercy and grace?
2. Have you led people to Christ or down an evil path?

TRIPPING OVER FLATTERY

Those who flatter their neighbors are spreading nets
for their feet (Proverbs 29:5).

F LATTERY is an insincere compliment. We are not to flatter but
to compliment others with sincerity. If we flatter people, we will
eventually trip over our words, as we are not telling the truth. Flattery
actually insults the other person because they probably know it isn't
true—or if they do believe your flattery, it may unjustly inflate their
ego. Always be sincere when complimenting someone—you will be
an encourager, and the person will be encouraged.

Points to Ponder

1. Have people flattered you? How did you feel?
2. Have you received sincere compliments? How did you feel?

DISCIPLINE AND ABUSE

Discipline your children, and they will give you peace; they will bring you the delights you desire (Proverbs 29:17).

THERE is much talk these days regarding child abuse—and rightly so. There is no excuse for abusing a child physically, emotionally, or verbally. Children are precious creations of God and they should be treated with tender loving care. Children need to be disciplined so they will mature into responsible, respectful adults. May the Lord guide every parent as they look only to God and His mercy and grace for the right way to correct their children.

Point to Ponder

1. If you are a parent, do you handle discipline according to God's commands?

UNCONTROLLED ANGER

An angry person stirs up conflict, and a hot-tempered person commits many sins (Proverbs 29:22).

A S the proverb states, an angry person stirs up conflict and a hot-tempered person commits many sins—that is a true statement that we all can agree on. At times in life, we become angry, and we may even react with a hot-temper depending on the situation. What makes the difference for believers who are upset—we have learned to control our anger and we don't sin because of our anger. Jesus was upset about what was going on in God's house, the temple. He vented His anger but did not hurt anyone and did not sin.

Point to Ponder

1. Are you able to control your anger and not sin?

_____

_____

_____

LOW VERSUS LOWLY

Pride brings a person low, but the lowly in spirit gain honor
(Proverbs 29:23).

PRIDE brings a person down—as it did with satan when tossed down out of Heaven. But people who are lowly in spirit—humble—will gain the heights of honor. Everyone suffers from being prideful from time to time. But what we do during those times is crucial. Immediately acknowledge pride, ask for forgiveness, and repent of it.

Points to Ponder

1. Do you battle bouts of pride?
2. Are you quick to toss it out and ask for forgiveness?

TWO THINGS I ASK

Two things I ask of you, Lord; do not refuse me before I die:
Keep falsehood and lies far from me; give me neither poverty
nor riches, but give me only my daily bread. Otherwise, I may
have too much and disown you and say, "Who is the Lord?"
Or I may become poor and steal, and so dishonor the name
of my God (Proverbs 30:7-9).

T HE request of the Lord seems right—that the man didn't want to hear any lies and he wanted to be fed every day. He didn't want to be tempted to abandon the Lord if had too many riches and he didn't want to dishonour the Lord by stealing if he was poor. May we be content with what the Lord has given us, may we never abandon Him or bring Him dishonour.

Points to Ponder

1. Do you find these two things odd that the man is asking of the Lord?

2. What are the two things you would ask for?

SPEAK UP

Speak up *for those who cannot speak for themselves, for the rights of all who are destitute.* **Speak up** *and judge fairly; defend the rights of the poor and needy* (Proverbs 31:8-9).

W E are called to speak for those who have no voice—in the government, the marketplace, the church—wherever people are being marginalized. We are called to speak up and judge fairly, defending the rights of the poor and needs. Although we may not be lawyers who speak up in courtrooms for these people, we can do our part in being active in our community and church. There are many organizations worldwide that are dedicated to helping others—participate with them or start your own.

Points to Ponder

1. Are you involved in outreach programs or organizations that help the poor?
2. Why or why not?

REPUTATION

A wife of noble character who can find? She is worth far more than rubies. Her husband has full confidence in her and lacks nothing of value. She brings him good, not harm, all the days of her life. ...Charm is deceptive, and beauty is fleeting; but a woman who fears the Lord is to be praised. Honor her for all that her hands have done, and let her works bring her praise at the city gate (Proverbs 31:10-31).

THIS passage from Proverbs 31 comprehensively details a "good wife." The description is quite thorough and I must say that it would be next to impossible for a woman, or a man for that matter, to be all these things all the time. It is, however, an excellent example of what we should aspire to, what we can aim for throughout our lives. Without an explanation of what an ideal person is, we have nothing on which to base our goals.

Point to Ponder

1. Does reading that passage (in its entirety) give you hope or does it discourage you? God meant it as an encouragement and an incentive to reach toward—start today!

CONTINUAL PRAYERS

*We always thank God for all of you and continually mention you in our prayers. We remember before our God and Father your work produced by **faith**, your labor prompted by **love**, and your endurance inspired by **hope** in our Lord Jesus Christ* (1 Thessalonians 1:2-3).

P AUL was writing to the church in Thessalonica, and the first thing he does is thank God for them and tells them that he *continually* prays for them. Then he goes into detail about the prayers. He specifically mentions faith, love, and hope—the foundation of God's good news message—with the greatest of these being love.

Points to Ponder

1. How often do you thank God for the people in your life?
2. The people in your church?
3. Your pastor?

October 16

IMITATORS

You became imitators of us and of the Lord, for you welcomed the message in the midst of severe suffering with the joy given by the Holy Spirit. And so you became a model to all the believers in Macedonia and Achaia (1 Thessalonians 1:6-7).

THE Thessalonians welcomed the good news of God while in the midst of *"severe suffering"*—being rewarded with joy from the Holy Spirit. They became the model for people throughout the region. Paul and others like him were eager to spread the news of Jesus' sacrifice so all could experience hope on earth and eternal life in Heaven.

Point to Ponder

1. Are you imitating Paul and the great men and women of the Bible who welcomed God's message and joy from the Holy Spirit?

THE WORD OF GOD

And we also thank God continually because, when you received the word of God, which you heard from us, you accepted it not as a human word, but as it actually is, the word of God, which is indeed at work in you who believe (1 Thessalonians 2:13).

P AUL continues to thank the Thessalonians because they accepted the word of God as from God. The people believed beyond what was being said by men to what God was saying to them. They received God's word and allowed it to settle within them.

Points to Ponder

1. How settled is the word of God within you?
2. Are you thankful for whoever shared the good news with you?
3. Have you thanked that person lately?

BLAMELESS AND HOLY

*May the Lord make **your love increase and overflow** for each other and for everyone else, just as ours does for you. May he **strengthen your hearts** so that you will be **blameless and holy** in the presence of our God and Father when our Lord Jesus comes with all his holy ones* (1 Thessalonians 3:12-13).

THE blessing that Paul bestowed upon the Thessalonians in these verses I bestow on you as well. That your love will increase and overflow for others, that God will strengthen your heart so you will be blameless and holy when Jesus returns.

Points to Ponder

1.   Are you looking forward to the day of Christ's return?
2.   Do you believe His return is imminent?

_____

_____

_____

CAUGHT UP TOGETHER

*For **the Lord himself will come down from heaven,** with a loud command, with the voice of the archangel and with the trumpet call of God, and **the dead in Christ will rise first.** After that, **we who are still alive and are left will be caught up together** with them in the clouds to meet the Lord in the air. And so **we will be with the Lord forever.** Therefore encourage one another with these words* (1 Thessalonians 4:16-18).

T HIS passage in the Bible has caused much discussion and various theories. Heated conversations have been sparked because of these two verses. Rather than being encouraging, as the writer intended, these words have caused contention and division within the church as a whole. Let's accept these words from God through Paul as encouragement and proof of God's return and our eternal life with Him in Heaven.

Points to Ponder

1. Have you been a participant in a discussion about "what these verses really mean"?

2. Do you know people who are adamant that they have the "right" interpretation of these verses?

GOD IS JUST

God is just: He will pay back trouble to those who trouble you and give relief to you who are troubled, and to us as well. This will happen when the Lord Jesus is revealed from heaven in blazing fire with his powerful angels. He will punish those who do not know God and do not obey the gospel of our Lord Jesus. They will be punished with everlasting destruction and shut out from the presence of the Lord and from the glory of his might (2 Thessalonians 1:6-9).

IN Paul's second letter to the church in Thessalonica, he tells them very bluntly about God's justice and what will happen to those who troubled God's children and to those who haven't accepted the gospel of Christ Jesus.

Point to Ponder

1. Does this final judgment motivate you to share the gospel with more fervor?

ONE PERSON

Go up and down the streets of Jerusalem, look around and consider, search through her squares. If you can find but one person who deals honestly and seeks the truth, I will forgive this city (Jeremiah 5:1).

GOD was willing to save the city if there was only one person who was dealing honestly and seeking the truth. Many of today's cities are full of dishonest and lying people. Believers must be a visible presence in every corner of the world. We must make our honest and truthful presence known in the community, the marketplace and business world, in hospitals, schools, and in our neighbourhoods. God wants none to perish.

Points to Ponder

1. Do you know people who are dealing honestly and seeking the truth?
2. Do you know people who are dishonest and denying the truth?
3. Which group has the greater number?

_____

_____

_____

STUBBORN AND
REBELLIOUS HEARTS

*But these people have stubborn and rebellious hearts;
they have turned aside and gone away. They do not say to
themselves, "Let us fear the Lord our God, who gives autumn
and spring rains in season, who assures us of the regular
weeks of harvest." Your wrongdoings have kept these away;
your sins have deprived you of good* (Jeremiah 5:23-25).

TOO often people succumb to stubborn and rebellious hearts—
their attitude causes them to turn away from God, to reject His
blessings. When we no longer respect Him and take His blessings for
granted, we are doing wrong and our sins will deprive us of all the
good things He wants to give us.

Points to Ponder

1. Is your heart beating with stubbornness and rebellion?
2. Or is your heart beating with thankfulness for God's
   blessings and eager to receive more goodness from
   Him?

HORRIBLE AND SHOCKING

A horrible and shocking thing has happened in the land: The prophets prophesy lies, the priests rule by their own authority, and my people love it this way. But what will you do in the end? (Jeremiah 5:30-31)

HORRIBLE and shocking things are happening in countries worldwide. Prophets are indeed prophesying lies, leaders are indeed ruling by their own authority, and the people accept these things! But what will we do in the end? What will be our excuses when the King of kings returns and demands an explanation?

Points to Ponder

1. What will you do in the end?
2. What will be your excuse when the King of kings returns and demands an explanation?

_____

_____

_____

REFORM REQUIRED

This is what the Lord Almighty, the God of Israel, says: **Reform your ways and your actions, and I will let you live in this place.** *Do not trust in deceptive words and say, "This is the temple of the Lord, the temple of the Lord, the temple of the Lord!" If you really change your ways and your actions and deal with each other justly, if you* **do not oppress the foreigner, the fatherless or the widow and do not shed innocent blood in this place, and if you do not follow other gods to your own harm, then I will let you live in this place**... (Jeremiah 7:3-6).

J EREMIAH told the people that they needed to change their ways and actions. They were not to trust in deceptive words and believe what they knew to be false. God is ready to receive all those who deal justly with each other and hold Him up as the only God.

Point to Ponder

1. Are there things in your life you need to change so you can live in your place—God's place of refuge and peace?

RESPECT

Do not rebuke an older man harshly, but exhort him as if he were your father. Treat younger men as brothers, older women as mothers, and younger women as sisters, with absolute purity (1 Timothy 5:1-2).

TREATING others with respect is an expected attitude for children of God. Older men and women deserve honor and gentle treatment. Young men and women are as our brothers and sisters, and our parents deserve our reverence. Men are to treat women with absolute purity and women are to treat men with respect. Many of today's television programs and movies show the opposite of these virtues, producing negative effects in our marriages, family relationships, and in many other areas of life. Let's change this trend—beginning in our own homes.

Point to Ponder

1. Are you willing to turn off the television and stop going to movies that advocate mistreatment of others?

SINGLE MOTHERS

Give proper recognition to those widows who are really in need. But if a widow has children or grandchildren, these should learn first of all to put their religion into practice by caring for their own family and so repaying their parents and grandparents, for this is pleasing to God. The widow who is really in need and left all alone puts her hope in God and continues night and day to pray and to ask God for help. But the widow who lives for pleasure is dead even while she lives (1 Timothy 5:3-6).

S OME very specific words are shared in this passage in First Timothy about widows, which I would also include single mothers as there are so very many of them these days. Unfortunately many children are growing up without fathers. We need to help these women and children as best we can.

Points to Ponder

1. Do you know single women who are having a hard time raising their children?
2. Are you in a position to help? With finances? Employment? Babysitting? Training?

_____

_____

_____

OBVIOUS AND TRAILING SINS

The sins of some are obvious, reaching the place of judgment ahead of them; the sins of others trail behind them. In the same way, good deeds are obvious, and even those that are not obvious cannot remain hidden forever (1 Timothy 5:24-25).

SOME people's sins are obvious to all who know them, others sins are hidden behind them and will only be evident when they are standing before God's throne of judgment. Likewise, our good deeds are usually obvious, but many we may not be aware of until God sheds light upon them on Judgment Day. We must never miss an opportunity to do good things for others.

Points to Ponder

1. Do you take pleasure in performing "random acts of kindness" that you may not get credit for?
2. Is your pleasure in giving rather than receiving?

GODLINESS WITH CONTENTMENT

*But **godliness with contentment is great gain.** For we brought nothing into the world, and we can take nothing out of it. But if we have food and clothing, we will be content with that. Those who want to get rich fall into temptation and a trap and into many foolish and harmful desires that plunge people into ruin and destruction. For **the love of money is a root of all kinds of evil.** Some people, eager for money, have wandered from the faith and pierced themselves with many griefs* (1 Timothy 6:6-10).

GODLINESS with contentment should be the goal of every believer. If we are content in living godly lives, there is no greater way to live. Being greedy for money and possessions brings the opposite of contentment—turmoil and destruction. Even believers have wandered from the faith in the pursuit of worldly riches. Let this not be so with us!

Point to Ponder

1. Are you pursuing a godly and contented life filled with the Lord's riches that will never rot or wither?

DO GOOD

*Command those who are rich in this present world not to be arrogant nor to put their hope in wealth, which is so uncertain, but to put their hope in God, who richly provides us with everything for our enjoyment. Command them to **do good**, to be rich in good deeds, and to **be generous and willing to share**. In this way they will lay up treasure for themselves as a firm foundation for the coming age, so that they may take hold of the life that is truly life* (1 Timothy 6:17-19).

THERE will always be rich people in the world—believers and unbelievers. God blesses His children with wealth in a variety of ways. But we are not to be arrogant or put our hope in worldly riches. Our hope must always be in the Lord only. We are to do good with our resources and lay up our riches in God's glory.

Points to Ponder

1. No matter your financial situation, there are always going to those worse off than you are.
2. Are you generous and willing to share with them?

A TRUSTWORTHY SAYING

Here is a trustworthy saying: If we died with him, we will also live with him, if we endure, we will also reign with him. If we disown him, he will also disown us; if we are faithless, he remains faithful, for he cannot disown himself (2 Timothy 2:11-13).

JESUS is a paradox that continues daily to amaze me with the magnitude of His love. He died so we could live; if we endure, He will allow us to share His majesty; if we disown Him, He will disown us; but if we lose faith in Him, He remains faithful to us.

Points to Ponder

1. Is it hard for you to understand the depth and breadth of how faithful and loving Jesus is?

2. Do you think you will ever comprehend Him this side of Heaven?

An Elder

An elder must be blameless, faithful to his wife, a man whose children believe and are not open to the charge of being wild and disobedient. Since an overseer manages God's household, he must be blameless—not overbearing, not quick-tempered, not given to drunkenness, not violent, not pursuing dishonest gain. Rather, he must be hospitable, one who loves what is good, who is self-controlled, upright, holy and disciplined. He must hold firmly to the trustworthy message as it has been taught, so that he can encourage others by sound doctrine and refute those who oppose it (Titus 1:6-8).

THE prerequisites for being an elder are appropriate for every member of God's Kingdom. These principles are worthy of our daily attention and focus. Conforming to this lifestyle brings not only honor upon ourselves but on our family and church as well—and to God's glory.

Point to Ponder

1. Do you agree that every member of God's household should be willing to aspire to the lifestyle described in the Scripture passage from Titus 1?

SALVATION FOR ALL

*For the grace of God has appeared that offers **salvation to all people.** It teaches us to **say "No" to ungodliness and worldly passions,** and to **live self-controlled, upright and godly lives** in this present age, while we wait for the blessed hope—the appearing of the glory of our great God and Savior, Jesus Christ, who gave himself for us to **redeem us** from all wickedness and to purify for himself **a people that are his very own, eager to do what is good*** (Titus 2:11-14).

WHILE we wait for our great God and Savior, Jesus Christ, to appear in all His glory, there are certain things we are supposed to do: say no to ungodliness and worldly passions; live self-controlled, righteous, and godly lives; and do what is good.

Points to Ponder

1. Do you say no to ungodliness and worldly passions?
2. Do you life a self-controlled, upright, and godly life?
3. Are you eager to do good?

_____

_____

_____

PARTNERSHIPS

*I pray that your partnership with us in the faith may be effective in **deepening your understanding** of every good thing we share for the sake of Christ. Your love has given me **great joy and encouragement**, because you, brother, have **refreshed the hearts** of the Lord's people* (Philemon 1:6).

FORMING partnerships with other believers is good—they are effective in deepening our understanding of His word. They also give great joy and encouragement and refresh our hearts. When we share ourselves with other believers, God is glorified.

Points to Ponder

1. Do you belong to a small group or attend a Bible study?
2. Do you attend Sunday school?
3. Do you regularly spend time with other believers?

HEIR OF ALL THINGS

In the past God spoke to our ancestors through the prophets at many times and in various ways, but in these last days he has spoken to us by his Son, whom he appointed heir of all things, and through whom also he made the universe. The Son is the radiance of God's glory and the exact representation of his being, sustaining all things by his powerful word. After he had provided purification for sins, he sat down at the right hand of the Majesty in heaven. So he became as much superior to the angels as the name he has inherited is superior to theirs (Hebrews 1:1-4).

JESUS is heir of all things. He is the radiance of God's glory and the exact representation of Him. Through Him we are purified for our sins. He sits beside God in Heaven and is our Mediator today and every day. God speaks to us through His Son—we need no other voice.

Points to Ponder

1.   Are you sustained by God's powerful word?
2.   Do you lean on God's appointed heir of all things?

MINISTERING ANGELS

To which of the angels did God ever say, "Sit at my right hand until I make your enemies a footstool for your feet"? Are not all angels ministering spirits sent to serve those who will inherit salvation? (Hebrews 1:13-14).

O NLY Jesus sits at the right hand of God the Father—not the angels. Angels have been charged with ministering to God's children—us—but we are not to show them more love or attention than God's only begotten Son, Jesus.

Points to Ponder

1. Has God sent an angel to assist you?
2. Have you seen an angel of God?

OUR GREAT AND AWESOME GOD

Do not be terrified by them, for the Lord your God, who is among you, is a great and awesome God. The Lord your God will drive out those nations before you, little by little. You will not be allowed to eliminate them all at once, or the wild animals will multiply around you. But the Lord your God will deliver them over to you, throwing them into great confusion until they are destroyed (Deuteronomy 7:21-23).

ONE thing I have come to realize is that success that you have not adequately prepared for can be more challenging than you can ever imagine. I have seen people's lives ruined and homes scattered because of a sudden explosion of success that could not be managed judiciously. Notice the wisdom of God in the above passage: *"drive out* [Israel's enemies] *little by little"* so that other issues or challenges, unbudgeted for, will not sneak in and overwhelm them. For example, some people who win lottery money are thrown into sudden financial abundance and become plagued with loss of values, saddled with mis-placed relational issues, and crippled with lack of priorities. God has you and all related concerns in His capable hands.

Points to Ponder

1. Are you prepared for the success God desires to give you?
2. Will you lose your values or change your priorities when you become successful?
3. How can you best prepare yourself?

FEAR THE LORD

Therefore, since **we have a great high priest who has ascended into heaven, Jesus the Son of God,** *let us hold firmly to the faith we profess. For we do not have a high priest who is unable to empathize with our weaknesses, but* **we have one who has been tempted in every way, just as we are—yet he did not sin.** *Let us then approach God's throne of grace with confidence, so that we may receive mercy and find grace to help us in our time of need* (Hebrews 4:14-16).

BECAUSE Jesus came to earth and become human, sacrificed Himself on our behalf, and then rose from the grave to sit on the right hand of God our Father, we can approach God's throne of grace with confidence—receiving mercy and grace whenever we are in need. Jesus, our Great High Priest and Mediator, can empathize with our weaknesses.

Points to Ponder

1. Do you walk confidently into His presence?
2. Does he shower you with mercy and grace during your time of need?

Reading the Bible in a Year: Jeremiah 43-45 and Hebrews 3.

FILLED WITH THE SPIRIT

During the days of Jesus' life on earth, he offered up prayers and petitions with fervent cries and tears to the one who could save him from death, and he was heard because of his reverent submission. Son though he was, he learned obedience from what he suffered and, once made perfect, he became the source of eternal salvation for all who obey him...
(Hebrews 5:7-9).

NEVER a day passed that Jesus didn't pray to His heavenly Father and for those He loved. He offered up his prayers and petitions with fervent cries and tears—and became our source of eternal salvation.

Points to Ponder

1. When was the last time you prayed with crying and tears?

2. Have you learned obedience from suffering that God allowed you to experience?

TO THE VERY END

We want each of you to show this same diligence to the very end, so that what you hope for may be fully realized. We do not want you to become lazy, but to imitate those who through faith and patience inherit what has been promised (Hebrews 6:11-12).

BELIEVERS must be diligent and hopeful until the end of our time on earth or until Jesus returns, whichever comes first. We are not to be lazy; we are to imitate those who have gone before us—those who were faithful and patient and received His promises to the full.

Points to Ponder

1. Are you committed to God to the very end of your days?
2. Will you be strong and faithful and patient, ready to step into your Promised Land?

Toward Maturity

Therefore let us move beyond the elementary teachings about Christ and be taken forward to maturity, not laying again the foundation of repentance from acts that lead to death, and of faith in God, instruction about cleansing rites, the laying on of hands, the resurrection of the dead, and eternal judgment (Hebrews 6:1-2).

MOVING forward into maturity brings new revelations about God and His mysterious ways. The more we study the word and ask the Holy Spirit for guidance, the more we grow up spiritually. This pleases God.

Point to Ponder

1. Are you moving forward toward spiritual maturity?

ONCE FOR ALL

Unlike the other high priests, he [Jesus] *does not need to offer sacrifices day after day, first for his own sins, and then for the sins of the people.* **He sacrificed for their sins once for all when he offered himself.** *For the law appoints as high priests men in all their weakness; but the oath, which came after the law, appointed* **the Son, who has been made perfect forever** (Hebrews 7:27-28).

JESUS became our High Priest, and His once-for-all sacrifice assures our place in eternity with Him.

Point to Ponder

1. What do these two verses in Hebrews 7 mean to you? Write your interpretation.

New Every Morning

*Because of **the Lord's great love** we are not consumed, for **his compassions never fail**. They are new every morning; **great is your faithfulness**. I say to myself, "The Lord is my portion; therefore I will wait for him" (Lamentations 3:22-24).*

WOE be to us if the Lord's great love is not present. Woe be to us if His compassions ever fail. Woe be to us if His faithfulness wasn't great. The Lord indeed is our portion and we must wait for Him, no matter how long He tarries to return.

Points to Ponder

1. Are you thankful every day that the Lord's great love keeps you from becoming consumed by the evilness of the world?

2. Do you wake each morning with a smile knowing that He is faithful to fulfill His promises?

DESTINED TO DIE ONCE

*Just as **people are destined to die once**, and after that to face judgment, so Christ was sacrificed once to take away the sins of many; and he will appear a second time, not to bear sin, but to bring salvation to those who are waiting for him* (Hebrews 9:27-28).

CONTRARY to some religions and soothsayers and psychics, the Bible teaches that people die and then face God's judgment. For those who believe that Jesus is the Son of God and have repented of their sins, there is no fear of death. Believers know that they will live eternally with the Trinity in Heaven—a place lovely beyond our imaginations.

Points to Ponder

1. Do you know people who believe in reincarnation?
2. Do you know people who think they can speak to the dead?
3. How do you interact with such people?

Reading the Bible in a Year: Ezekiel 1-3 and Hebrews 9.

HIS COVENANT

The Holy Spirit also testifies to us about this. First he says: "This is the covenant I will make with them after that time, says the Lord. I will put my laws in their hearts, and I will write them on their minds." Then he adds: "Their sins and lawless acts I will remember no more." And where these have been forgiven, sacrifice for sin is no longer necessary (Hebrews 10:15-18).

HAVING God's laws in our hearts and minds is the best way to stay in God's will for our lives, for we will be constantly reminded about doing and saying the right things. And knowing that He will forget about our sins and disobedience should make us ever so grateful.

Points to Ponder

1. Do you appreciate having God's laws absorbed within you?
2. Do they help you make the right decisions?

LET US CONSIDER

And let us consider how we may spur one another on toward love and good deeds, not giving up meeting together, as some are in the habit of doing, but encouraging one another—and all the more as you see the Day approaching (Hebrews 10:24-25).

THE writer of Hebrews is encouraging believers to reach out to other believers in love and with good deeds. He reemphasizes the importance of meeting together and encouraging each other. Then he hints at the approaching "Day."

Points to Ponder

1. Are you considering how you can spur others on toward love and good deeds?

2. Are you meeting together with other believers, encouraging them?

3. What "Day" do you think is being referenced?

BY FAITH

By faith Noah, when warned about things not yet seen, in holy fear built an ark to save his family. By his faith he condemned the world and became heir of the righteousness that is in keeping with faith (Hebrews 11:7).

THE expression *"by faith"* is used frequently in Hebrews 11 describing many well-known biblical men and women. By faith they did remarkable things for God and by God's direction. Without faith, it is impossible to please God (Heb. 11:6).

Point to Ponder

1.   How is your faith growing? Sporadically or consistently?

By Faith, Again

By faith the people passed through the Red Sea as on dry land; but when the Egyptians tried to do so, they were drowned. By faith the walls of Jericho fell, after the army had marched around them for seven days (Hebrews 11:29-30).

F AITH in God and His ultimate plan for us is what separates Christians from others. Without faith in His supreme and perfect will for our lives, we would easily fall prey to the devil's lies and temptations. Without faith in His sustaining love, we would rely instead on drugs or alcohol or sexual perversion for consolation. Faith is your purchasing power in the realm of the spirit; it cushions you from the elements of present circumstances and connects you with the joyful expectation of what lies ahead.

Point to Ponder

1. Is your faith strong enough to keep you from stumbling into the devil's snares?

THOUSANDS OF ANGELS

But you have come to Mount Zion, to the city of the living God, the heavenly Jerusalem. You have come to thousands upon thousands of angels in joyful assembly, to the church of the firstborn, whose names are written in heaven. You have come to God, the Judge of all, to the spirits of the righteous made perfect (Hebrews 12:22-23).

THE writer of Hebrews describes Mount Zion as the city of the living God, the heavenly Jerusalem, where thousands of joyful angels are assembled. There the living God is Judge of all and there our spirits will be made perfect.

Points to Ponder

1. Doesn't Mount Zion sound like a wonderful place?
2. What will it be like when your spirit is made perfect?

Love and Hospitality

*Keep on **loving one another** as brothers and sisters. Do not forget to **show hospitality** to strangers, for by so doing some people have shown hospitality to angels without knowing it. Continue to **remember those in prison** as if you were together with them in prison, and those who are mistreated as if you yourselves were suffering* (Hebrews 13:1-3).

WHEN you love and show hospitality to people, you will be pleasing God—you may even be entertaining angels! God sends His angels to do His bidding on earth, and sometimes He may use them to test you. Also, we are to remember those who are unjustly sent to prison. Even today, many Christians worldwide are imprisoned because of their beliefs. Keep them in your prayers—remember them as if you were being mistreated for your faith.

Points to Ponder

1. Do you think you have hosted an angel in disguise?
2. Do you remember persecuted Christians in your prayers?

KEEP SABBATHS HOLY

*I am the Lord your God; follow my decrees and be careful to keep my laws. **Keep my Sabbaths holy,** that they may be a sign between us. Then you will know that I am the Lord your God* (Ezekiel 20:19-20).

S UNDAY used to be a special day of the week. People would crowd into churches on Sundays; stores used to be closed on Sundays; families would sit down at the table and after thanking God for their food, would eat a meal together. Sundays used to mean no work, no gambling, no worldliness—a total focus on God. But all that has changed in many societies and countries, and even many churches.

Points to Ponder

1. Do you purposely keep the Lord's day special, sacred?
2. Or is Sunday just like any other day for you, for your family?

SPECIAL ATTENTION FOR ALL

My brothers and sisters, believers in our glorious Lord Jesus Christ **must not show favoritism.** *Suppose a man comes into your meeting wearing a gold ring and fine clothes, and a poor man in filthy old clothes also comes in. If you show special attention to the man wearing fine clothes and say, "Here's a good seat for you," but say to the poor man, "You stand there" or "Sit on the floor by my feet," have you not discriminated among yourselves and become judges with evil thoughts?*
(James 2:1-4)

WE are told not to discriminate—every person who comes to our church or ministry or home should be received with the same amount of respect. In fact, we should give everyone special attention who is seeking God's presence.

Points to Ponder

1. Have you witnessed discrimination at your church?
2. Your workplace?
3. What is your reaction?

A FIERY TONGUE

Likewise, the tongue is a small part of the body, but it makes great boasts. Consider what a great forest is set on fire by a small spark. **The tongue also is a fire, a world of evil** *among the parts of the body. It corrupts the whole body, sets the whole course of one's life on fire, and is itself set on fire by hell* (James 3:5-6).

OUR tongue, our speech, can get us into much trouble. If we are not careful what we say, our words can cause great harm—as deadly as an out-of-control forest fire. Even more, what we say can change the entire course of our lives and send us to a place of sorrow.

Point to Ponder

1. Do you make it a habit to think before you speak, just in case what you say may be hurtful or reflect negatively on yourself or your heavenly Father?

ENMITY AGAINST GOD

You adulterous people, don't you know that friendship with the world means enmity against God? Therefore, anyone who chooses to be a friend of the world becomes an enemy of God (James 4:4).

J AMES makes it very clear that believers can't be in a relationship with the world and love God at the same time. An adulterer is married to a person but is having a relationship with someone other than the spouse. This is not permitted in marriage and it is not permitted regarding our relationship with the world and God.

Point to Ponder

1. What does the following phrase mean to you? You are to be in the world but not of the world.

_____

_____

_____

RICH PEOPLE

Now listen, you rich people, weep and wail because of the misery that is coming on you. Your wealth has rotted, and moths have eaten your clothes. Your gold and silver are corroded. Their corrosion will testify against you and eat your flesh like fire. You have hoarded wealth in the last days. Look! The wages you failed to pay the workers who mowed your fields are crying out against you. The cries of the harvesters have reached the ears of the Lord Almighty. You have lived on earth in luxury and self-indulgence. You have fattened yourselves in the day of slaughter. You have condemned and murdered the innocent one, who was not opposing you (James 5:1-6).

A S mentioned in a previous day, God does not oppose believers being wealthy, but He does oppose haughty attitudes, greed, and selfishness. And if your riches cause you to have these attitudes, then your wealth is causing you to be on the wrong side of God.

Point to Ponder

1. Do you know people who are stingy with the wealth God gave them?

LIVING HOPE

Praise be to the God and Father of our Lord Jesus Christ! In his great mercy he has given us new birth into a living hope through the resurrection of Jesus Christ from the dead, and into an inheritance that can never perish, spoil or fade... (1 Peter 1:3-4).

WHAT an wonderful phrase and reality—*"living hope"!* Unlike other religions, Christians have *"living hope through the resurrection of Jesus Christ from the dead."* Hallelujah! Our God is alive and living within us.

Points to Ponder

1. What does living hope mean to you?
2. Are you eager to claim your inheritance that will never perish, spoil, or fade?

ABSTAIN FROM SINFUL DESIRES

Dear friends, I urge you, as foreigners and exiles, to abstain from sinful desires, which wage war against your soul. Live such good lives among the pagans that, though they accuse you of doing wrong, they may see your good deeds and glorify God on the day he visits us (1 Peter 2:11-12).

A S we resist sinful desires and live good lives among unbelievers, we will be living examples of God's mercy and grace. People will see the good things we do and they will know that God is the One who empowers us to be kind and generous.

Points to Ponder

1. Are you a living example of God's mercy and grace?
2. Do you do good deeds for His glory so others will come to know Him?

_____

_____

_____

THE VALUE OF INNER BEAUTY

Wives, in the same way submit yourselves to your own husbands so that, if any of them do not believe the word, they may be won over without words by the behavior of their wives, when they see the purity and reverence of your lives. Your beauty should not come from outward adornment, such as elaborate hairstyles and the wearing of gold jewelry or fine clothes. Rather, it should be that of your inner self, the unfading beauty of a gentle and quiet spirit, which is of great worth in God's sight (1 Peter 3:1-4).

ALTHOUGH this passage of Scripture is directed to wives, it is just as appropriate for people in general. (In fact, in this day and age, many men are just as conscious about their appearance as women.)

Point to Ponder

1. Are you more concerned with the purity of your inner self than your outward adornment?

THE END OF ALL THINGS

*The end of all things is near. Therefore **be alert and of sober mind** so that you may **pray**. Above all, **love each other deeply**, because love covers over a multitude of sins. **Offer hospitality** to one another without grumbling. Each of you should **use whatever gift you have received to serve others,** as faithful stewards of God's grace in its various forms* (1 Peter 4:7-10).

A S this age comes to an end, Peter advises us to be alert and sober. He tells us to pray, love each other deeply, be hospitable without grumbling, and to use our gifts to serve others. This is good advice for today and every day until the end of time.

Point to Ponder

1. As a faithful steward of God's grace, are you following Peter's advice?

_____

_____

_____

RESIST AND STAND FIRM

Be alert and of sober mind. Your enemy the devil prowls around like a roaring lion looking for someone to devour. Resist him, standing firm in the faith, because you know that the family of believers throughout the world is undergoing the same kind of sufferings (1 Peter 5:8-9).

AGAIN Peter tells us to be alert and sober. When we are not alert and sober, the devil can easily devour us. He is always ready to slip into someone's life when they are inattentive or drunk. Drunkenness causes people to stumble. So, resist the devil with a clear mind and stand firm in your faith!

Points to Ponder

1. Are you usually alert and mindful of the devil's attempts to overpower you?

2. Do you stand firm in your faith and resist him?

DIVINE NATURE

Through these he has given us his very great and precious promises, so that through them you may participate in the divine nature, having escaped the corruption in the world caused by evil desires (2 Peter 1:4).

W E have escaped corruption caused by evil desires because of the promises of God, including our participation in His divine nature. As long as we focus on God and obey Him, we will not be corrupted by the world.

Point to Ponder

1. What does it mean to you to be a participant in His divine nature?

_____

_____

_____

FALSE PROPHETS AND TEACHERS

But there were also false prophets among the people, just as there will be false teachers among you. They will secretly introduce destructive heresies, even denying the sovereign Lord who bought them—bringing swift destruction on themselves. Many will follow their depraved conduct and will bring the way of truth into disrepute. In their greed these teachers will exploit you with fabricated stories. Their condemnation has long been hanging over them, and their destruction has not been sleeping (2 Peter 2:1-3).

PLEASE be aware of false teachers who try to sway you with destructive heresies. We must not allow those who deny the sovereignty of the Lord to infiltrate the church and exploit the Lord's word. Ask God for discernment and that the Holy Spirit would identify false prophets and teachers.

Points to Ponder

1. Have you witnessed false teachings?
2. What was your reaction?

SCOFFERS

Above all, you must understand that in the last days scoffers will come, scoffing and following their own evil desires. They will say, "Where is this 'coming' he promised? Ever since our ancestors died, everything goes on as it has since the beginning of creation." But they deliberately forget that long ago by God's word the heavens came into being and the earth was formed out of water and by water. By these waters also the world of that time was deluged and destroyed. By the same word the present heavens and earth are reserved for fire, being kept for the day of judgment and destruction of the ungodly (2 Peter 3:3-7).

EVEN in biblical time, centuries ago, Peter had to warn people about the same scoffers we have to deal with today. Thankfully we can use his response to wave off unbelievers who don't know that God's word is forever—unchanging and true.

Points to Ponder

1. Have you had to deal with people who scoff at God's word?

2. Were you successful in getting your point across and defending the word of God?

SCOFFERS BEWARE

But do not forget this one thing, dear friends: With the Lord a day is like a thousand years, and a thousand years are like a day. The Lord is not slow in keeping his promise, as some understand slowness. Instead he is patient with you, not wanting anyone to perish, but everyone to come to repentance (2 Peter 3:8-9).

E VEN though scoffers have been around for centuries making fun of God's word, He includes them in the plan for everyone to come to repentance and not perish. Our God is an amazing, forgiving God who gives second chances to those we think are undeserving. God's love is beyond our comprehension.

Point to Ponder

1. Are you confident that God will keep His promises?

_____

_____

_____

LIVE LIKE JESUS

We know that we have come to know him if we keep his commands. Whoever says, "I know him," but does not do what he commands is a liar, and the truth is not in that person. But if anyone obeys his word, love for God is truly made complete in them. This is how we know we are in him: Whoever claims to live in him must live as Jesus did (1 John 2:3-6).

W E are obviously Christians if we keep His commandments. The Ten Commandments are the foundation of a godly life— the life that Jesus lived.

Point to Ponder

1. Have you read the Ten Commandments lately?

SIN NO MORE

*No one who is born of God will continue to sin, because God's seed remains in them; they cannot go on sinning, because they have been born of God. This is how we know who the children of God are and who the children of the devil are: **Anyone who does not do what is right is not God's child,** nor is anyone who does not love their brother and sister* (1 John 3:9-10).

I F we are born of God we will stop sinning. To sin is to remain in the world. We know who the children of God are because they do what is right. The children of the devil do not love. Therefore, love others as God commands.

Points to Ponder

1. Are you born of God?
2. Do you love His children?

THE ONE WITHIN IS GREATER

*You, dear children, are from God and have overcome them, because **the one who is in you is greater than the one who is in the world*** (1 John 4:4).

THIS is a favorite verse for many Christians. As long as we remember that the Holy One who lives in us is greater than the devil of the world, we can rest assured that nothing the devil can scheme will harm us.

Points to Ponder

1. Is this one of your favorite verses?
2. What are a few more verses that bring you comfort or give you strength? Write them below.

HIM WHO IS TRUE

We know that we are children of God, and that the whole
world is under the control of the evil one. We know also that
the Son of God has come and has given us understanding, so
that we may know him who is true. And we are in him who is
true by being in his Son Jesus Christ. He is the true God and
eternal life (1 John 5:9-20).

A S children of God, we know that the world is controlled by the evil one that God tossed out of Heaven. We also know from reading Scripture that God gives us understanding so that we will know what is true and false.

Points to Ponder

1. Are you confident as a child of God?
2. Do you have understanding of truth?

_____

_____

_____

WHILE PRAYING

While I was speaking and praying, confessing my sin and the sin of my people Israel and making my request to the Lord my God for his holy hill—while I was still in prayer, Gabriel, the man I had seen in the earlier vision, came to me in swift flight about the time of the evening sacrifice. He instructed me and said to me, "Daniel, I have now come to give you insight and understanding. As soon as you began to pray, a word went out, which I have come to tell you, for you are highly esteemed (Daniel 9:20-23).

G OD will send us insight and understanding—just as He did for Daniel. All we have to do is pray, confess our sin, and wait. God may send an angel, another person, a sign of some sort; He has various ways to communicate with us. Be ready to receive.

Points to Ponder

1. Has God used an angel to give you a message?
2. In what ways have you heard His voice?

NO GREATER JOY

Dear friend, I pray that you may enjoy good health and that all may go well with you, even as your soul is getting along well. It gave me great joy when some believers came and testified about your faithfulness to the truth, telling how you continue to walk in it. I have no greater joy than to hear that my children are walking in the truth (3 John 2-4).

I T is kind to pray for our friends, that they will enjoy good health. John was pleased and filled with *"great joy"* when he heard that his friends were being faithful to the truth and continuing to walk in God's way. The same is true when our friends become believers and our children and grandchildren. There really isn't any greater joy than to know our loved ones are believers and walking in the light of God's glory.

Point to Ponder

1. Have you experienced the joy of knowing that your friends and family are walking in the Truth?

_____

_____

_____

PERVERSION AND DENIAL

For certain individuals whose condemnation was written about long ago have secretly slipped in among you. They are ungodly people, who pervert the grace of our God into a license for immorality and deny Jesus Christ our only Sovereign and Lord (Jude 1:4).

THERE were certain ungodly individuals who slipped in among the church, and they were perverting the grace of God into permitting immorality and denying Jesus as God's only Son. This false teaching continues to spread like a cancer within the church even today. We must be discerning and have no part of this perversion and denial of our Lord Jesus Christ.

Points to Ponder

1. Are you aware of this type of teaching?
2. Did it spread or was it stopped?

I AM

I am the Alpha and the Omega," says the Lord God, "who is, and who was, and who is to come, the Almighty (Revelation 1:8).

THIS proclamation by the Lord is all-encompassing. He is stating emphatically that He is the One True God. There are no others. He was before the beginning and He will remain after the end. He is our Almighty God.

Point to Ponder

1.   Write in your own words what this statement means to you.

_____

_____

_____

YOUR FIRST LOVE

I know your deeds, your hard work and your perseverance. I know that you cannot tolerate wicked people, that you have tested those who claim to be apostles but are not, and have found them false. You have persevered and have endured hardships for my name, and have not grown weary. Yet I hold this against you: You have forsaken the love you had at first (Revelation 2:2-4).

ALTHOUGH the church at Ephesus was commended for their deeds, hard work, and perseverance, they were reprimanded because they had forsaken their first love—their hot and passionate love for God. They had fallen away from the deeply personal love they first had for Him.

Points to Ponder

1. Has your love for God waned?
2. Is it time to rekindle the fire in your heart for Him?

HOT, COLD, OR LUKEWARM?

I know your deeds, that you are neither cold nor hot. I wish you were either one or the other! So, because you are lukewarm—neither hot nor cold—I am about to spit you out of my mouth (Revelation 3:15-16).

IN John's revelation, the church in Laodicea was told that they were lukewarm and that the Lord was about to spit them out of His mouth. He would rather them be either cold or hot—either for Him or against Him. Being lukewarm is being neutral—standing for nothing on either side.

Point to Ponder

1. Are you spiritually hot, cold, or lukewarm?

_____

_____

_____

HOLY, HOLY, HOLY

Each of the four living creatures had six wings and was covered with eyes all around, even under its wings. Day and night they never stop saying: "'Holy, holy, holy is the Lord God Almighty,' who was, and is, and is to come" (Revelation 4:8).

G OD is worthy to be praised every moment of every day— which is what was revealed to John. When we are ushered into Heaven when our days are completed here on earth, we too will join the choirs of angels and creatures praising and singing of His glory.

Points to Ponder

1. Have you read the book of Revelation?
2. Is it intriguing or baffling?

WORTHY IS THE LAMB

Then I looked and heard the voice of many angels, numbering thousands upon thousands, and ten thousand times ten thousand. They encircled the throne and the living creatures and the elders. In a loud voice they were saying: "Worthy is the Lamb, who was slain, to receive power and wealth and wisdom and strength and honor and glory and praise!"
(Revelation 5:11-12).

AGAIN, there is praising in Heaven. There were so many angels that John was unable to count them all—yet they had one purpose and one loud voice saying the same thing, *"Worthy is the Lamb, who was slain, to receive power and wealth and wisdom and strength and honor and glory and praise!"*

Point to Ponder

1. Do you think we have to wait until we get to heaven to join the thousands of angels and the other creatures in praising the Lamb of God?

Five-Day Prayer and Fasting
Day One

FOR the next five days, I encourage you to fast—sacrifice—something you enjoy to show your devotion to God. Today's Scripture focus to pray on is: *"The race is not to the swift or the battle to the strong, nor does food come to the wise or wealth to the brilliant or favor to the learned; but time and chance happen to them all"* (Ecclesiastes 9:11).

Points to Ponder

1. What are you going to fast from?
2. Why is this fast special to you?
3. What does this Scripture passage mean to you?

FIVE-DAY PRAYER AND FASTING
DAY TWO

F OR the next four days, I encourage you to fast—sacrifice—something you enjoy to show your devotion to God. Today's Scripture focus to pray on is: *"You have searched me, Lord, and you know me. You know when I sit and when I rise; you perceive my thoughts from afar"* (Psalm 139:1-2).

Points to Ponder

1. What are you going to fast from?
2. Why is this fast special to you?
3. What does this Scripture passage mean to you?

_____

_____

_____

FIVE-DAY PRAYER AND FASTING
DAY THREE

F OR the next three days, I encourage you to fast—sacrifice—something you enjoy to show your devotion to God. Today's Scripture focus to pray on is: *"For you created my inmost being; you knit me together in my mother's womb. I praise you because I am fearfully and wonderfully made; your works are wonderful, I know that full well"* (Psalm 139:13-14).

Points to Ponder

1.   What are you going to fast from?
2.   Why is this fast special to you?
3.   What does this Scripture passage mean to you?

FIVE-DAY PRAYER AND FASTING
DAY FOUR

FOR the next two days, I encourage you to fast—sacrifice—something you enjoy to show your devotion to God. Today's Scripture focus to pray on is: *"If only you, God, would slay the wicked! Away from me, you who are bloodthirsty! They speak of you with evil intent; your adversaries misuse your name"* (Psalm 139:19-20).

Points to Ponder

1. What are you going to fast from?
2. Why is this fast special to you?
3. What does this Scripture passage mean to you?

PRAYER AND FASTING
DAY FIVE

TODAY, I encourage you to fast—sacrifice—something you enjoy to show your devotion to God. Today's Scripture focus to pray on is: *"Search me, God, and know my heart; test me and know my anxious thoughts. See if there is any offensive way in me, and lead me in the way everlasting"* (Psalm 139:23-24).

Points to Ponder

1. What are you going to fast from?
2. Why is this fast special to you?
3. What does this Scripture passage mean to you?

THE HIGHEST OF
THE MOUNTAINS

*In the last days the mountain of the Lord's temple will be
established as the highest of the mountains; it will be exalted
above the hills, and peoples will stream to it (Micah 4:1).*

THERE is talk about the last days throughout the Bible, which
was written centuries ago. No one knows when Jesus will return,
but we must be aware that He could appear any minute. We must live
and work, planning for the future, but always with our faces toward
the heavens anticipating His imminent return.

Points to Ponder

1. Have you heard the many people who predict the end of
   the world?

2. What motivates these people when the Bible clearly
   states that the time is unknown even to God's own Son?

GLORY AND HONOR AND POWER

Then war broke out in heaven. Michael and his angels fought against the dragon, and the dragon and his angels fought back. But he was not strong enough, and they lost their place in heaven. The great dragon was hurled down—that ancient serpent called the devil, or Satan, who leads the whole world astray. He was hurled to the earth, and his angels with him
(Revelation 12:7-9).

MANY people don't understand all that is written in the book of Revelation. The book of Revelation is the book of the future church, the book of the acts of the angels and of cosmic involvement in the affairs of the earth. But we must have faith that in God's perfect timing, He will reveal what we need to know concerning the wars and the creatures and the activities within the heavens.

Points to Ponder

1. Are you eager to understand the stories told in Revelation?
2. Or are you content knowing that all will be revealed in God's good time?

Vengeance Is the Lord's

The Lord is a jealous and avenging God; the Lord takes vengeance and is filled with wrath. The Lord takes vengeance on his foes and vents his wrath against his enemies. The Lord is slow to anger but great in power; the Lord will not leave the guilty unpunished (Nahum 1:2-3).

WE need not concern ourselves with being vengeful, because the Lord is a jealous and avenging God. He will take vengeance on His foes and will avenge wrongs done to His children.

Points to Ponder

1. Are you quick to anger and to inflict revenge?
2. Or are you slow to anger and willing to let God be your avenger?

THE NEW JERUSALEM

Then I saw "a new heaven and a new earth," for the first heaven and the first earth had passed away, and there was no longer any sea. I saw the Holy City, the new Jerusalem, coming down out of heaven from God, prepared as a bride beautifully dressed for her husband (Revelation 21:1-2).

THE new Jerusalem will be perfectly adorned to be placed within the new heaven and new earth. In Revelation, there are many visions. Trust in God from Genesis through Revelation. The Holy Spirit will help you understand all that is true.

Points to Ponder

1. Are you prepared for whatever God has in store for you?
2. For the world?

NO MORE DEATH OR PAIN

*He [God] will wipe every tear from their eyes. There will be
no more death or mourning or crying or pain, for the old
order of things has passed away. He who was seated on the
throne said, "I am making everything new!" Then he said,
"Write this down, for these words are trustworthy and true."
He said to me [John]: "It is done. I am the Alpha and the
Omega, the Beginning and the End. To the thirsty I will give
water without cost from the spring of the water of life. Those
who are victorious will inherit all this, and I will be their God
and they will be my children* (Revelation 21:4-7).

IMAGINE a world with no more tears, where there is no more
mourning. Those who are thirsty will drink from the spring of the
water of life. Victory is assured. The word of God is true and trustworthy—and we are His children forevermore.

Points to Ponder

1. How hard is it for you to imagine a world like this?
2. Are you ready to embrace such a world?

_____

_____

_____

IMMANUEL—GOD WITH US

*Therefore the Lord himself will give you a sign: The virgin will
conceive and give birth to a son, and will call him Immanuel.
He will be eating curds and honey when he knows enough to
reject the wrong and choose the right* (Isaiah 7:14-15).

THE birth of Jesus was foretold in Isaiah. And indeed a virgin,
Mary, did conceive and give birth to a son. As he grew, he knew
right from wrong and with divine guidance from the Holy Spirit, we
can make the right choices throughout our lives as well.

Point to Ponder

1. There are those who doubt that Jesus is the Son of God
    born of a virgin. How do you respond to this type of
    skepticism?

GREETINGS!

*The angel went to her and said, "**Greetings, you who are highly favored! The Lord is with you.**" Mary was greatly troubled at his words and wondered what kind of greeting this might be. But the angel said to her, "**Do not be afraid, Mary; you have found favor with God. You will conceive and give birth to a son, and you are to call him Jesus. He will be great and will be called the Son of the Most High. The Lord God will give him the throne of his father David, and he will reign over Jacob's descendants forever; his kingdom will never end**" (Luke 1:28-33).*

MARY must have been startled initially by the angel's appearance. Then she was comforted by the angel's command not to be afraid. After the angel told Mary about conceiving and giving birth to the Son of the Most High, no doubt she was bewildered. Nonetheless, she accepted what the angel told her.

Points to Ponder

1. Do you readily accept things you don't understand?
2. What do you think your reaction would be if confronted by an angel with a life-changing message from God?

DO NOT BE AFRAID

*And there were shepherds living out in the fields nearby, keeping watch over their flocks at night. An angel of the Lord appeared to them, and the glory of the Lord shone around them, and they were terrified. But the angel said to them, "**Do not be afraid.** I bring you **good news** that will cause great joy for all the people* (Luke 2:8-10).

AGAIN an angel appeared, and this time the shepherds were afraid—even terrified! But the angel told them not to be afraid. This angel was bringing *"good news that will cause great joy for all the people."* Jesus became flesh and blood so *all* people would experience great joy and eternal life.

Points to Ponder

1. Have you shared the joy of Christmas with people of other faiths?

2. Why or why not?

GLORY TO GOD IN THE HIGHEST!

For there is born to you this day in the city of David a Savior, who is Christ the Lord. And this will be the sign to you: You will find a Babe wrapped in swaddling cloths, lying in a manger." And suddenly there was with the angel a multitude of the heavenly host praising God and saying: "Glory to God in the highest, and on earth peace, goodwill toward men!" (Luke 2:11-14 NKJV).

THE name of Jesus continues to bring hope—and horror—to millions of people. This baby wrapped in blankets and placed in a feed trough introduced a new era of God's reign in the world. His presence would be felt by everyone who came in contact with Him—and continues to affect all those who hear the good news of the gospel.

Point to Ponder

1. Will you join the angels by singing "Glory to God in the highest, and on earth peace, goodwill toward all"?

JESUS—THE LIGHT OF THE WORLD

So they [the shepherds] *hurried off and found Mary and Joseph, and the baby, who was lying in the manger. When they had seen him, they spread the word concerning what had been told them about this child, and all who heard it were amazed at what the shepherds said to them. But Mary treasured up all these things and pondered them in her heart. The shepherds returned, glorifying and praising God for all the things they had heard and seen, which were just as they had been told* (Luke 2:16-20).

THE shepherds didn't just stand around thinking about what the angel told them. No, they hurried off to find the baby who would change the world. The baby who would heal crippled people, make blind men see, resist the devil's temptations, feed a multitude with barely enough to feed a family. The shepherds glorified and praised God for all they had heard and seen—supernaturally realizing the magnitude of this little child's birth.

Point to Ponder

1. Can you see yourself hurrying off to welcome Jesus when He returns the second time?

SALVATION AND REVELATION

Simeon took him in his arms and praised God, saying: "Sovereign Lord, as you have promised, you may now dismiss your servant in peace. For my eyes have seen your salvation, which you have prepared in the sight of all nations: a light for revelation to the Gentiles, and the glory of your people Israel (Luke 2:28-32).

S IMEON realized that Jesus was the promised Deliverer. He knew that God had sent Jesus as the long-awaited Messiah, the salvation of the world, the light of revelation to the Jews and the Gentiles alike. He praised God—as should we daily.

Points to Ponder

1. Do you celebrate Christ throughout the year?
2. Is He your focus at Christmas time rather than the other so-called symbols of the season?

ANOTHER YEAR!

*One day I walked by the field of an old lazybones, and then passed the vineyard of a lout; they were overgrown with weeds, thick with thistles, all the fences broken down. I took a long look and pondered what I saw; **the fields preached me a sermon** and I listened...* (Proverbs 24:30-34 The Message)

G OD speaks to us in many ways—through other people, events, and even nature. In the above passage, the writer says what he saw "preached" message to him. *"Then I beheld and considered it well; I looked and received instruction"* (Prov. 24:32 AMP) and *"I looked at this, thought about it, and learned a lesson from it"* (Prov. 24:32 Good News Bible). God can speak to you through your everyday life experiences. As the last day of the year, please *"take a long look and ponder"* what God has taught you throughout the year. Has it been a good year? Use this time to turn your past struggles into opportunities for practical and positive actions. Not sure of what tomorrow holds? Remember, humanity is limited, but God is unlimited. Change will come and today will turn into tomorrow—and God always makes the difference. Enter the New Year with hope and determination. It is the joyful expectation of what the future holds that enhances our victory over doubts and gives us the zeal to face another new day! *With God, you will not fail!*

Points to Ponder

1. Do you welcome each New Year with prayers of thankfulness and gratitude for God's unfailing love and grace?

Reading the Bible in a Year: Malachi and Revelation 22.

Praying the Word in Every Situation

PROPHETIC PRAYER POINTS

Please Pray

1. Pray to break any generational vow of poverty: *"His father Isaac answered him, 'Your dwelling will be away from the earth's richness, away from the dew of heaven above. ...But when you grow restless, you will throw his yoke from off your neck'"* (Gen. 27:39-40). Esau broke the curse. Esau asked, *"What's the meaning of all these flocks and herds I met?" "To find favor in your eyes, my lord,"* he said. But Esau said, *"I already have plenty, my brother. Keep what you have for yourself"* (Gen. 33:8-9).

2. Refuse to be called names that connote pain, misery, sorrow, or poverty, *"By faith Moses, when he had grown up, refused to be known as the son of Pharaoh's daughter"* (Heb. 11:24).

3. Pray for your family and your children, Malachi 2:15 says, *"Has not the one God made you? You belong to him in body and spirit. And what does the one God seek? Godly offspring."*

Declare Your Trust in God

1. Put your trust in God. *"As for God, his way is perfect; the word of the LORD is tried: he is a buckler to all them that trust in him"* (2 Sam. 22:31 KJV). *"The LORD is my rock, and my fortress, and my deliverer; my God, my strength,*

in whom I will trust; my buckler, and the horn of my salvation, and my high tower" (Ps. 18:2 KJV). *"Some trust in chariots, and some in horses: but we will remember the name of the LORD our God"* (Ps. 20:7 KJV). *"The LORD redeemeth the soul of his servants: and none of them that trust in him shall be desolate"* (Ps. 34:22 KJV).

2. *"But upon mount Zion shall be deliverance, and there shall be holiness; and the house of Jacob shall possess their possessions. And the house of Jacob shall be a fire, and the house of Joseph a flame, and the house of Esau* [your enemies] *for stubble, and they shall kindle in them, and devour them..."* (Obadiah 17-18 KJV).

3. The devil has no right over what the Lord has given you (see Judg. 11:23-24). *"And they rose up in the morning early, and worshipped before the LORD, and returned, and came to their house to Ramah: and Elkanah knew Hannah his wife; and the LORD remembered her"* (1 Sam. 1:19 KJV).

Pray Against Willful Sins:

Pray Psalm 19:13, *"Keep your servant also from willful sins; may they not rule over me"* and Psalm 119:133: The Dangers of Willful Sins: The Sins of Ahab

1. Ahab knowingly committed the sins of Jeroboam and caused Israel to sin.

2. He married Jezebel, the daughter of Ethbaal, king of the Sidonians.

3. He served and worshiped Baal.

4. He built an altar for Baal in Samaria.

5. He also made Asherah poles.

6. May the sins of Ahab not rule over you.

Pray that You will Fulfill Your Purpose in Your Generation - Acts 13:36

Pray that you will leave a mark for future generations no matter your life circumstances. Omri left a mark for his posterity:

1. He eliminated the initial opposition of Tibni.

2. Captured more territories from Moab.

3. Stopped the advancing Assyrian power.

4. Built the new capital, Samaria.

5. Assyria regarded Israel as the house of Omri.

6. But he followed the way and sins of Jeroboam.

7. Omri was succeeded by Ahab, his son.

The Power of Unity
Pray for unity in your congregation.

There are many instances in the Bible of the display of the power of unity. Unity has power that should be put to godly use. One of these godly uses is recorded in the Old Testament, *"...as the trumpeters and singers **were as one,** to make one sound to be heard in praising and thanking the LORD..."* (2 Chron. 5:13 KJV). The result was that the temple was filled with God's palpable glory!

And in the book of Acts of the Apostles, we see another power demonstration of unity, *"...they raised their voices together in prayer to God..."*; the result, *"...the place where they were meeting was shaken and they were all filled with the Holy Spirit and spoke the word of God boldly"* (Acts 4:24,31).

Sometimes, people put the power of unity into wrong and ungodly purposes:

Now the whole earth had one language and one speech. And it came to pass, as they journeyed from the east, that they found a plain in the land of Shinar, and they dwelt there. Then they said to one another, "Come, let us make bricks and bake them thoroughly." They had brick for stone, and they had asphalt for mortar. And they said, "Come, let us build ourselves a city, and a tower whose top is in the heavens; let us make a name for ourselves, lest we be scattered abroad over the face of the whole earth." But the LORD came down to see the city and the tower which the sons of men had built. And the LORD said, "Indeed the people are one and they all have one language, and this is what they begin to do; now nothing that they propose to do will be withheld from them. Come, let Us go down and there confuse their language, that they may not understand one another's speech." So the LORD scattered them abroad from there over the face of all the earth, and they ceased building the city. Therefore its name is called Babel, because there the LORD confused the language of all the earth; and from there the LORD scattered them abroad over the face of all the earth (Genesis 11:1-10 NKJV).

Today, I have an idea: why don't you bring some people into unity with you and raise your voices in praises and in prayers! There is no telling what He can do through you.

Pray that God will Bring Deliverance and Blessings

1. God will bring deliverance, *"And everyone who calls on the name of the LORD will be saved; for on Mount Zion and in Jerusalem there will be deliverance"* (Joel 2:32a).

2. Blessings! Blessings! *"'Yes indeed, it won't be long now.' God's Decree. 'Things are going to happen so fast your head will swim; one thing fast on the heels of the other. You won't be able to keep up. Everything will be happening at once and everywhere you look blessings! Blessings like wine pouring off the mountains and hills. I'll make everything right again for my people Israel: They'll rebuild their ruined cities. They'll plant vineyards and drink good wine. They'll work their gardens and eat fresh vegetables. And I'll plant them; plant them on their own land. They'll never again be uprooted from the land I've given them.' God, your God, says so"* (Amos 9:13-15 The Message).

Pray for God's Vindication and Justice

1. Vindication and justice will flow from Heaven to bring you to your destiny, *"But let justice roll on like a river, righteousness like a never-failing stream!"* (Amos 5:24).

2. Restoration of the tabernacle of David is in your midst—praise will not cease from your house, *"I will restore David's fallen shelter—I will repair its broken walls and*

restore its ruins—and will rebuild it as it used to be"
(Amos 9:11).

Please Pray

Please pray along the following lines:

1. That doors will no longer be shut against you; Isaiah 45:1 says, *"...so that gates will not be shut."*

2. That great and effective door to be opened unto you for your ministry, job, finances, and family (see 1 Cor. 16:5-9).

3. Grace to become first among equals, *"the king found them ten times better"* than their equals (see Dan. 1:20).

4. None of us shall miss *the set time*. *"Now Elizabeth's full time came..."* (Luke 1:57 KJV) and she gave birth to baby boy; this is she who was called barren.

5. Every "Marah" situation shall be turned into sweetness (see Exod. 15:22-24).

6. Pray that the Word of God will greatly increase in your surrounding area and many will turn back to the faith.

Declare that the Will of God will Prevail

1. The Lord will cause *"the omens of boasters to fail, making fools out of diviners..."* (Isa. 44:25 NASB).

2. The Lord will fulfill His promises in your life (see Isa. 44:26).

3. He will quench the evil fiery darts (see Eph. 6:16).

4. The Word of God will break to pieces every rock of resistance, offense, failure, shame, and reproach (see Jer. 23:29).

5. The Lord will break any unholy soul-tie in your life just as Moses *"refused to be called son of Pharaoh's daughter"* (Heb. 11:24 NKJV).

6. Pray for the presence of God, *"For the earth will be filled with the knowledge of the glory of the Lord as the waters cover the sea"* (Hab. 2:14). This is a divine promise!

7. In Exodus 33:16 Moses says, *"What else will distinguish me and your people from all the other people on the face of the earth?"* His presence!

8. For fresh release of the *tongues of fire* as was on the day of Pentecost, His presence will birth new depths of God in your life (see Acts 2).

Please Pray

"LORD, I have heard of your fame; I stand in awe of your deeds, LORD. Repeat them in our day, in our time make them known; in wrath remember mercy" (Hab. 3:2). May the Lord ignite the greatness within you. Pray for reawakening in your life, your church, your ministry.

1. Pray for divine contact, divine appointment and assignment (see 2 Sam. 9:2-11).

2. Break any soul-tie to any unholy ancestral attachment. See Hebrew 11:24 when Moses refused to be called son of Pharaoh's daughter.

3. Pray for a life full of "days and years." Abraham died an old man and full of years (see Gen 25:7); Job also died old and full of days (see Job 42:16). May your days and years count before God. That is what counts most!

4. May you not be given the wrong label—say to whatever force *"count not thine handmaid for a daughter of Belial* [wickedness]*"* (1 Sam. 1:16 KJV).

Unison Prayer

It is always an honor to pray in unison with people who are committed to God! Samuel said, *"Far be it from me to sin against the Lord by failing to pray for you"* (1 Sam. 12:23).

Pray along these lines:

1. God will send us *"help from the sanctuary"* (Ps. 20:2 NKJV); *"the Lord is my Helper"* (Heb. 13:6 NKJV); help will come *"from another place"* (Esther 4:14).

2. Any demon-inspired or man-made drought or famine is hereby abolished. The siege is lifted! (See 2 Kings 7:1.)

In twenty-four hours, abundance will replace drought in your life.

3. The glorious presence of God will continue to be upon and guide you in all undertakings (see Exod. 40:34-38).

4. The tongues of fire of the Holy Spirit, as in the day of Pentecost, will rest on you and cause divine transformation in your life (see Acts 2:1-2).

Pray for Divine Protection

1. *"God is jealous over those whom He loves, that is why He takes vengeance on those who hurt them"* (Nahum 2:2 Living Bible). Pray for divine protection that God will be jealous over your life and make your enemies His enemies.

2. Pray for your city or region using Second Kings 2:19-22 (NKJV), *"This city is pleasant...but the water is bad"*; therefore pray that God will heal the city and heal every area of unproductiveness.

3. Psalm 102:13 says that the Lord will arise and show you favor for your set time, a time has come.

4. Pray for protection in the season of the *"official celebration of witchcraft"* (Halloween) using Psalm 91 and Numbers 23:23.

Serious Prayer Time

It is wise to take prayer time seriously. Please pray along these lines:

1. From limitation to fullness in God, *"He also brought me up out of a horrible pit, out of the miry clay and set my feet upon a rock and established my steps. He has put a new song in my mouth..."* (Ps. 40:2-3 NKJV).

2. That the Lord will be your strong tower, *"When my heart is overwhelmed; lead me to the rock that is higher than I. For You have been a shelter for me, a strong tower from the enemy"* (Ps. 61:2-3 NKJV).

3. *"The lines have fallen to me in pleasant places. Yes, I have a good inheritance"* (Ps. 16:6 NKJV).

4. Pray for your pastor using Colossians 4:12.

Pray as You Walk

Pray as you walk with the Lord! That the following will be done in your life:

1. Isaiah 58:6
   - to loose the bonds of wickedness and chains of injustice;
   - untie the cords of the heavy work;
   - to let the oppressed go free;
   - to break every yoke.

2. Use the principles of Psalm 32:1-2 to ensure no deceit is in your spirit.

3. Use Psalm 32:5-9 to remove hindrances to gaining understanding of your walk and relationship with God.

4. Pray for all God's projects, that God would help from His sanctuary.

Prophetic Word about Fasting

Fasting is a form of deliberate self-denial. It is a sacrificial form of yielding yourself to deeper things of God's spirituality in your life. It enhances the human spirit while bringing the body and soul to the subjection of Jesus Christ. A three-day fast is reminiscent of Esther's fast, and it is still as powerful today as it was then. Fasting reduces the influence of your flesh (carnal nature) and enhances your spirit. Fasting brings your spirituality up to a new level in God.

Fast and prayer for five days using the following Bible verses:

- Luke 19:29-31; *loose it and bring it here and because the Lord has need of it.*
- Isaiah 66:9; the Lord is able to bring delivery when He brings you to a place of birth.
- Ezra 1:1; the Lord will stir up the spirit of those involved in the process to release the money without delay.

- Job 20:15; to vomit up the funds as God will cast the money out of His belly (any delaying agent in the process).
- Jeremiah 20:9; any delaying agent can no longer hold it back and it will be like fire shut up in his heart and bones.

Prayers Never Fail

Pray for:

- Miraculous multiplication. John 6:9: *"Here is a boy with five small barley loaves and two small fish, but how far will they go among so many?"*
- Open heavens; visions of God; the Word to come expressly; and the good hand of God to be with you (see Ezek. 1:3). Second Samuel 16:11-12 says that God will turn the curse of Shimei into blessings; pray for God to grant vengeance for all injustice and that the Shimei curse and pains will be the trigger for God to help you.
- God to speak to you from the place of mercy, from the place of atonement, and from the place of the power of testimony (see Num. 7:89).
- God to bless you; to enlarge your coast; to be with you; to keep you from evil, and that you will be a blessing to others (1 Chron. 4:10, the Prayer of Jabez).

Prayers of Sanctification

The need to call a holy fast and declare a period of sanctification should always be a priority as long as humankind lives in our earthen vessels. For sanctification, use the following:

1. Psalm 119:133 (NKJV), *"let no iniquity have dominion over me."*
2. You are washed by the blood of Jesus.
3. Joshua 3:5 (NKJV), *"Sanctify yourselves, for tomorrow the Lord will do wonders among you."*
4. Second Chronicles 29:5 (NKJV), *"Hear me Levites! Now sanctify yourselves, sanctify the house of the Lord God of your fathers and carry out the rubbish from the holy place."*

Pray for His Power in Your Life

Using Zechariah 3 and 4, pray the following:

- Rebuke every work, conspiracy, or gathering of the enemy against you and the church of Christ, *"the Lord said to Satan, "The Lord rebuke you, Satan!"* (Zech. 3:2 NKJV).

- Ask God to take away all filthy garments so you will be covered by the richness of His glorious clothing (see Zech. 3:4).

- Pray that you will begin to possess your possessions like the sons of Jacob on Mount Zion.

- Pray for divine advancement (see 1 Sam. 12:6 KJV and 1 Kings 18:46).

- *"Not by might nor by power, but by My Spirit, says the Lord Almighty"* (Zech. 4:6).

- Our hands will complete what Your hands have started. *"Do not despise these small beginnings"* (see Zech. 4:10).

- There will be continuous supply of the anointing and power of God in our lives.

- Now the Lord will have mercy and do something amazing for you and among you.

- *"Blow the trumpet in Zion, declare a holy fast, call a sacred assembly;...bring together the elders, gather the children, those nursing at the breast. Let the bridegroom leave his room and the bride her chamber"* (Joel 2:15-16). Then surely, the Lord will repay you for the years the locusts have eaten (see Joel 2:25).

- Also pray using Joshua 3:5 and Psalm 51.

Pray for open heavens using Ezekiel 1:1-3. Now I declare upon you that you are ready to punish every form of disobedience.

Pray for the Threshing Floor Experience
(see 2 Sam. 24:16,21-25)

The threshing floor of Araunah was a place for: mercy, compassion, forgiveness, threshing (separation of substance from chaffs, crucifying the flesh and releasing the spirit), and sacrifice. It was the place Abraham attempted to sacrifice Isaac and the place also that Solomon built the magnificent temple of God.

1. Pray to break the bond of wickedness using Isaiah 58:6 (NKJV), *"Is this not the fast that I have chosen: to loose the bonds of wickedness; to undo the heavy burdens; to let the oppressed go free; and that you break every yoke?"*

2. Pray for purification, sanctification, and consecration using Joshua 3:5, *"Sanctify yourselves for tomorrow the Lord will do wonders among you."*

3. Pray for the healing of the land and the water that lies beneath the ground using Second Kings 2:19-22.

4. Pray to become a vessel of honor in the hands of God using Second Timothy 2:20, Ephesians 5:3-4, and Ephesians 3:14-19.

5. Pray that the Lord of breakthrough will break out ahead of you as you enter a new day, week, month, and year. David said, *"As waters break out, God has broken out against my enemies by my hand"* (1 Chron. 14:11b).

6. The blessings of the ark of God will rest upon you and your family:

   • In the midst of a national closed Heaven, Samuel stayed with the ark and the heavens opened upon him (see 1 Sam. 3:3-4).

   • In the midst of national fear, Obed-Edom received the ark and he and everything he had were blessed (see 1 Chron. 13:14).

7. Bless your family; *"David returned home to bless his family"* (1 Chron. 16:43).

8. The blessings of obedience will rest on you throughout the years (Lev. 26:3-13).

Please Pray

Please continue to pray as led by the Holy Spirit and also pray along these lines:

1. That the Lord would stretch out His hands to heal and perform miraculous signs in your midst (Acts 4:24-31).

2. That *"your days of sorrow will end"* (Isa. 60:20) and the spirit of misery banished from your midst.

3. That the spirit of near-success is cast out—this is also the spirit of Pisgah (the mountain where Moses saw the Promised Land but did not enter). You will both see and enter into the promises of God in your life (see Deut. 34:1,4).

4. That the spirit of hostility (the mark of Ishmael) is cast out of your life (see Gen. 16:12). For you are of the line of the child of promise, not of the slave woman.

5. That failure and delay will be far from you (see 1 Sam. 30:7-8; Ezek. 12:28)—no more delay.

Focus Passages

It is good to focus on Scripture that will hoist you into the spirit realm where God resides. Believe that:

1. You will witness the opening of ancient gates (see Ps. 24:7-10); and that the iron gate will open on its own (see Acts 12:10).

2. The Breaker's anointing will break out ahead of you (see Micah 2:13).

3. God will arise and His enemies will be scattered (see Ps. 68:1).

4. It is time for God to act, His laws will not be broken (Ps. 119:106).

5. The blessings of Joseph rest upon you; the best of the earth and sun, finest of the moon, and the fruitfulness of the everlasting hills (Deut. 33:13-18).

Prayers Make a Difference

Your prayers make a difference in your life, the lives of others, and in the world. Pray that:

1. The lamp of God shall continue to burn in your life (see Lev. 24:2-4).

2. The Lord will provide you a feast of rich food and a banquet of aged wine on His mountain (Isa. 25:6).

3. Light will break forth for you even in dark places, and your righteousness will break out like the dawn of new day (Ps. 37:6).

4. God will send help from His sanctuary to your home and region (Ps. 20:1-4).

5. There will be an adjustment to every *"inharmonious circumstances and conditions"* in your life (Eccl. 12:13b AMP).

6. You will enjoy the fruit of your righteousness (see Ezek. 34:25-29).

This Is the Time

1. This is the time of your favor, the set time, and the time to favor Zion has come (see Ps. 102:13).

2. May your family and ministry be exalted above of the intrigues of humankind—the mountain of the Lord shall become the chief mountain (see Micah 4:1-4).

3. You shall be like those who were in Goshen during the plagues in Egypt; excepted from the economic recession, protected and blessed by God (see Exod. 9:3-6; 10:25-26).

God's Promises

Pray that:

1. None of God's promises concerning you shall fail (see Josh. 21:2-4).

2. The Lord will grant you a word and wisdom that none can refute (John 21:15).

3. God will raise up believers in your community as the army of God. David's army was like the army of God (see 1 Chron. 12:23).

4. God will bless and give the earth another chance as He did by rescuing and blessing Noah and his family. May God bless you with Noah's blessings (see Gen. 9:1-3).

Prophetic Prayer Focus

1. *"God has spoken once, twice have I heard this: all power belongs to God"* (Ps. 62:11 NKJV). This is confidence!

2. That you will know the power of His resurrection in your life more than ever before (see Phil. 3:10).

3. That God will order your steps (see Ps. 37:23) and His word will be the lamp to show you the way to go (see Ps. 119:105).

4. That God will send atonement for you so that any impending judgment or calamity will be averted (see Num. 16:46-48). Every "strange fire" will be put off, no matter how it was put on.

5. That God will open the windows of Heaven and pour out His blessings upon you (see Mal. 3:10). Every "waster" will be rebuked for you.

6. That God will send resources for your needs.

Know Him and His Power

Pray that:

1. You may know Him and the power of His resurrection (see Phil. 3:10); you will enjoy the power of His resurrection in a new and fresh way.

2. The mountain of the Lord's temple will be established chief among the mountains—raised above the hills, and people will stream to it (see Micah 4:1). May the plans of God prevail over all other plans.

3. On Mount Zion you will possess your possessions.

4. God will encompass you with His favor (see Ps. 5:12): He is your shield, the glory and the lifter up of your head (see Ps. 3:3). He will bring you to a spacious place; keep your lamp burning, turn your darkness into light so you can advance against a troop and leap over a wall (see Ps. 18:19-29).

Your God

Know that:

1. Your God will always be near you, *"...our God is near us whenever we pray to Him"* (Deut. 4:7).

2. You are blessed by God, no one can reverse that blessing, *"I have received a command to bless; he has blessed and I cannot change it. No misfortune is seen in Jacob, no misery observed in Israel. The Lord their God is with them..."* (Num. 23:20-21).

3. A thousand-fold increase will be your portion, *"May the Lord God of your fathers make you a thousand times more numerous than you are, and bless you as He has promised you!"* (Deut. 1:11 NKJV).

4. You will conquer and possess the land, *"See I have begun to deliver Sihon and his country over to you. Now begin to conquer and possess his land"* (Deut. 2:31).

5. God, your God, will destroy the spirit of Jezebel (see Rev. 2:20-23).

Please Pray

1. Pray Psalm 20:1-2 (NKJV), *"May the LORD answer you in the day of trouble; may the name of the God of Jacob defend you; may He send you help from the sanctuary, and strengthen you out of Zion."*

2. May God remember all your sacrifices and may He give you the desires of your heart and make your plans succeed (see Ps. 20:4).

3. That you may testify that the Lord saves His anointed and He answers you from His holy Heaven with the saving power of His right hand (see Ps. 20:6).

4. *"My times are in your hands; deliver me from the hands of my enemies, from those who pursue me,"* (Ps. 31:15). In the shelter of His presence He will hide you from the intrigues of others and in His dwelling He will keep you safe from accusing tongues (see Ps. 31:20).

5. You will have victories everywhere you go (see 1 Chron. 18:6,13).

Your Best Is Yet to Come

1. Love and unity will reign in your family and in your midst. Psalm 133:3 says, *"there the Lord bestows his blessing, even life forevermore."*

2. His good promises over your life shall not be delayed any longer. Ezekiel 12:28 says there will be no more delay.

3. The Lord will give you the oil of joy instead of mourning and the garment of praise instead of the spirit of heaviness (see Isa. 61:3).

4. Waters will burst forth in the wilderness and streams in the desert (see Isa. 35:6).

5. Declare the blessings of the Trinity that Apostle Paul taught, *"May the grace of the Lord Jesus Christ, and the love of God, and the fellowship of the Holy Spirit be with you all"* (2 Cor. 13:14) and plead the blood of Jesus at all times!

Your best is yet to come as you continue to trust in the Lord.

Prayer Points from Joshua 21:43-45

1. Pray that you receive all your blessings, *"So the LORD gave Israel all the land he had sworn to give their ancestors, and they took possession of it and settled there."*

2. Pray that you have rest on all sides, "The Lord gave them rest on every side" that you will enjoy righteousness, joy, and peace in the Holy Spirit. Every war will cease!

3. Pray that all who rise up against you shall submit to you, "Not one of their enemies withstood them."

4. Pray that your destiny will be realized! Not one single promise of God concerning you will fail, *"Not one of all the LORD's good promises to Israel failed; every one was fulfilled."*

Prayer Points from Psalm 20

Pray that:

1. God will always answer you, "May the Lord answer you."

2. God will send you help, "May He send you help from the sanctuary."

3. The Lord will remember your sacrifice, "May He remember all your sacrifices."

4. God will grant your request, *"May the Lord grant all your requests."*

5. God will give you your desires and make your plans succeed, *"May He give you the desire of your heart and make all your plans succeed."*

6. That you will come to the true realization, *"know that the Lord gives victory to His anointed."*

Please Pray

1. Pray for the adjustment of every inharmonious circumstance (see Eccl. 12:13 AMP) to the original purpose of God!

2. Pray for purification and consecration, *"But in a great house there are not only vessels of gold and silver, but also* [utensils] *of wood and earthenware, and some for honourable and noble* [use] *and some for menial and ignoble* [use]. *So whoever cleanses himself* [from what is ignoble and unclean, who separates himself from contact with contaminating and corrupting influences] *will* [then himself] *be a vessel set apart and useful for honourable and noble purposes, consecrated and profitable to the Master, fit and ready for any good work"* (2 Tim. 2:20-21 AMP) and *"But immorality (sexual vice) and all impurity of lustful, rich, wasteful* [living] *or greediness must not even be named among you, as is fitting and proper among saints (God's consecrated people)"* (Eph. 5:3 AMP).

3. Waiting with patience upon the Lord to renew your strength, *"He gives strength to the weary and increases the power of the weak. Even youths grow tired and weary, and young men stumble and fall; but those who hope in the LORD will renew their strength. They will soar on*

wings like eagles; they will run and not grow weary, they will walk and not be faint" (Isa. 40:29-31).

4. Moving into overflow anointing, *"You prepare a table before me in the presence of my enemies. You anoint my head with oil; my cup overflows"* (Ps. 23:5).

5. Love and blessings—pray that God's blessings will continue to fill your life with an abundance of love and happiness always. May the love of God continue to be shared abroad in your heart! *"And hope does not put us to shame, because God's love has been poured out into our hearts through the Holy Spirit, who has been given to us"* (Rom. 5:5).

This concludes our time of refreshing together—please know that God is always on your side, always ready to bring you comfort, healing, and joy. We hope you have enjoyed discovering the treasures within and will refer to it often during times of thankfulness or troubles. Remember, hope is only a prayer away.

A PLACE OF LOVE AND REFRESHMENT
AT THE HEARTBEAT OF
ABERDEEN

THE FATHER'S HOUSE
Spreading the love of the Father abroad

Unveiling the Treasure in earthen vessels

www.the-fathers-house.org.uk

CONTACT INFORMATION

For additional copies of this book and other products from Cross House Books, contact: sales@crosshousebooks.co.uk.

Please visit our Website for product updates and news at www.crosshousebooks.co.uk.

OTHER INQUIRIES

CROSS HOUSE BOOKS
Christian Book Publishers
245 Midstocket Road, Aberdeen, AB15 5PH, UK

info@crosshousebooks.co.uk
publisher@crosshousebooks.co.uk

"The entrance of Your Word brings light."

Do you want to become a published author
and get your book distributed worldwide
by major book stores?

Contact:
admin@crosshousebooks.co.uk
www.crosshousebooks.co.uk.
or write to
CROSS HOUSE BOOKS
245 Midstocket Road, Aberdeen, AB15 5PH, UK

NEW TITLES FROM
CROSS HOUSE BOOKS

Growing God's Kingdom

Written by an experienced Bible scholar and beloved pastor, the insights and depth of God's word is thoughtfully shared so that newborn Christians and mature believers alike can understand and appreciate. Prefaced with an intriguing prophecy, *Growing God's Kingdom* contains practical principles that reveal the importance of God's mandate to share the gospel. You will learn about being mentored and mentoring those next in line to inherit God's riches.

40 Names of the Holy Spirit

The names of God represent a deliberate *invitation to you* to take advantage of what God can and wants to be in your life. Whatever you call Him is what He will become to you. Do you know all of His names? How much deeper would you like to know the Comforter? You will learn: Seven Symbols of the Holy Spirit; Names of the Holy Spirit; Seven Things *Not* to Do to the Holy Spirit; Twentyfold Relationship with the Holy Spirit; Fourfold Presence of the Holy Spirit; Seven Keys to Receiving the Holy Spirit Baptism—and much more!

Destined for the Top

Destined for the Top presents simple and proven successful answers to life's most complex questions. Divided into two parts—Life Issues and Family Issues—you can be at the top of your game in every aspect of your life by knowing what and who to avoid during your journey to the top. Through an added feature of thought-provoking questions at the end of each chapter, you will learn how to strengthen your spirit, invest in your potential, and realize how fickle your feelings really are. You will discover how God's wisdom and love through you propels you toward fulfilling your destiny!

Times of Refreshing Volume 1

Times of Refreshing allows you to tap in to daily super-natural experiences! Overflowing with inspiring mes-sages, comforting prayers, and Scriptures that bring His presence to you, these daily boosts of God's love are just what the Doctor ordered for a healthy mind, body, and spirit. Best-selling author and Pastor Bishop Joe Ibojie and Pastor Cynthia Ibojie bring 365 days of hope and refreshment into your personal space.

BOOKS BY DR. JOE IBOJIE

How to Live the Supernatural Life in the Here and Now—BEST SELLER

Are you ready to stop living an ordinary life? You were meant to live a supernatural life! God intends us to experi-ence His power every day! In *How to Live the Supernatural Life in the Here and Now* you will learn how to bring the supernatural power of God into everyday living. Finding the proper balance for your life allows you to step into the supernatural and to move in power and authority over everything around you. Dr. Joe Ibojie, an experienced pas-tor and prolific writer, provides practical steps and instruction that will help you live a life of spiritual harmony.

Dreams and Visions Volume 1—BEST SELLER

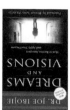

Dreams and Visions presents sound scriptural principles and practical instructions to help you understand dreams and visions. The book provides readers with the necessary understanding to approach dreams and visions by the Holy Spirit through biblical illustrations, understanding of the meaning of dreams and prophetic symbolism, and by exploring the art of dream interpretation according to ancient methods of the Bible.

Dreams and Visions Volume 2—NEW

God speaks to you through dreams and visions. Do you want to know the meaning of your dreams? Do you want to know what He is telling and showing you? Now you can know! *Dreams and Visions Volume 2* is packed full of exciting and Bible-guided ways to discover the meaning of your God-inspired, dreamy nighttime adventures and your wide-awake supernatural experiences!

Illustrated Bible-Based Dictionary of Dream Symbols—BEST SELLER

Illustrated Bible-Based Dictionary of Dream Symbols is much more than a book of dream symbols. This book is a treasure chest, loaded down with revelation and the hidden mysteries of God that have been waiting since before the foundation of the earth to be uncovered. Whether you use this book to assist in interpreting your dreams or as an additional resource for your study of the Word of God, you will find it a welcome companion.

EXPANDED AND ENRICHED
WITH EXCITING NEW CONTENT
Bible-Based Dictionary of Prophetic Symbols
for Every Christian—NEW

The most comprehensive, illustrated Bible-based diction-ary of prophetic and dream symbols ever compiled is contained in this one authoritative book! *The Bible-Based Dictionary of Prophetic Symbols for Every Christian* is a masterpiece that intelligently and understandably bridges the gap between prophetic revelation and application—PLUS it includes the expanded version of the best selling *Illustrated Bible-Based Dictionary of Dream Symbols*.

The Justice of God: Victory in Everyday Living—NEW

Only once in awhile does a book bring rare insight and godly illumination to a globally crucial subject. This book is one of them! A seminal work from a true practitioner, best-selling author, and leader of a vibrant church, Dr. Joe Ibojie brings clarity and a hands-on perspective to the Justice of God. *The Justice of God* reveals: How to pull down your blessings; How to work with angels; The power and dangers of prophetic acts and drama.

The Watchman: The Ministry of the Seer in the Local Church—NEW

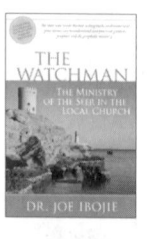

The ministry of the watchman in a local church is possibly one of the most common and yet one of the most misunderstood ministries in the Body of Christ. Over time, the majority of these gifted people have been driven into reclusive lives because of relational issues and confusion surrounding their very vital ministry in the local church.

Korean translations:
Dreams and Visions Volume 1

Italian translation:
Dreams and Visions Volume 1

The Final Frontiers—Countdown to the Final Showdown

The Final Frontiers—Countdown to the Final Showdown peers profoundly into the future. It expertly explores the emerging cosmic involvement of the seemingly docile elements of nature and their potential to completely alter the ways of warfare. Christians must not allow the things that are supposed to bless them to become instruments of judgment or punishment. *The Final Frontiers* provides you with a practical approach to the changing struggles that confront humanity now and in your future.